D1159902

The Shannon Sailors

Also by Leonard Wibberley

Mrs. Searwood's Secret Weapon
Stranger at Killnock
The Quest of Excalibur
Take Me to Your President
McGillicuddy McGotham
Beware of the Mouse
The Mouse That Roared
The Mouse on the Moon
The Mouse on Wall Street
A Feast of Freedom
The Island of the Angels
The Hands of Cormac Joyce
The Road from Toomi
Adventures of an Elephant Boy
The Centurion
Meeting with a Great Beast

NONFICTION

Voyage by Bus
Ah Julian!
Yesterday's Land
Towards a Distant Land
No Garlic in the Soup
The Land That Isn't There

JUVENILES (FICTION)

Deadmen's Cave
Kevin O'Connor and the Light Brigade
The Wound of Peter Wayne
John Treegate's Musket
Peter Treegate's War
Sea Captain from Salem
Treegate's Raiders
Leopard's Prey

JUVENILES (NONFICTION)

Wes Powell—Conqueror of the Colorado
The Life of Winston Churchill
John Barry—Father of the Navy
The Epics of Everest
Man of Liberty—the Life of Thomas Jefferson
Young Man from the Piedmont
A Dawn in the Trees
The Gales of Spring
Time of the Harvest

ATLANTIC

OCEAN

Londonderry

NORTHERN

IRELAND

Belfast

Sligo

IRISH
SEA

Connemara

Carrick
on Shannon
Lough Boderg
L. Bofin
Lough Forbes
Termonbarry
Longford
Lanesborough

Lough
Ree

Galway

Athenry

Athlone

Grand Canal

Liffey

Dublin

Philipstown
Tullamore

Shannon
Banagher

Portumna

The
Wicklows

Lough Derg
Garrykennedy
Killaloe
Nenagh

Shannon
Airport

Shannon

R. Shannon

Mouth of the
Shannon

Churruby
Limerick

Tipperary

Killarney

Cork

IRELAND

0   10   20   30   40   50
Miles

Leonard Wibberley The Shannon Sailors

A Voyage to the Heart of Ireland

William Morrow & Company, Inc., New York / 1972

The Shannon Sailors

Chapter 1

I was born in Ireland and in Dublin, which is a city where beautiful white swans once glided on the river in the middle of the town and where you may leave a bicycle untended and unchained on the main street (a beautiful gold and red bicycle with the greatest appeal) and return to find it untouched five hours later.

I don't remember much about Dublin in my childhood, except a glimpse of the sea, smooth and green as jade, at Blackrock or thereabouts. I remember Cork better, where we lived in a house opposite the Common, which seemed always to be flooded with rainwater and where I caught many leopard frogs at great peril. They had lovely little golden tints in their eyes, and it was easy to see in the elegance of a frog that they were all of them princes bewitched. Bewitched or not, it was held a dangerous thing in my childhood to have your mouth open and a frog in your hands, for he would certainly pop down inside you and you would die in a moment. In Ireland, according to childhood lore, more children are destroyed by frogs jumping about in their vitals than are carried off by eagles in Switzerland or turned into stones in Norway by the horrid glance of a troll. Yet there is a great elegance to frogs and, if you were to take an impartial look at a frog and at a lemur, for example, you could not but decide that evolution had taken the wrong path.

It was to show Ireland, the place of my birth, to my

sons that I took my voyage through Ireland last year. My
sons are all Americans, born and raised in western America,
and there is then between us not only that generation gap
which God in His wisdom put between Adam and his
children, but also a cultural gap. We are come from differ-
ing though not inimical soil. I wanted them to know my
roots as I know theirs.

I have four sons. The year of my own venture, the eldest,
Kevin, twenty, had already taken off for the Old World
on his own to glory in the roses of Spain and marvel at the
snake charmers of Algiers. He, then, was to meet me at
Shannon Airport, and I sent a message to him to that
effect at Biarritz, at Paris, and at Antwerp, for Americans
do not realize, as do Europeans, that these places are very
far apart, and scarcely to be visited in the same year. He
visited them all in the same week, and my message finally
reached him in London. Kevin was named both for St.
Kevin of Glendalough and for Kevin Barry, who was
hanged November 1, 1920, at the age of eighteen for taking
part in the Irish Revolutionary War.

My second son, Christopher, seventeen, is named after
that saint, beloved of all Christians, who carried Christ
across a river. The Church has recently expressed some
doubts as to whether St. Christopher ever existed, but the
doubts refer to mortal existence. That he has existed for
centuries in the minds and prayers of the faithful is beyond
any question whatever, and the matter of his physical
existence is purely academic. Reality is not bound up in
flesh and blood and tangible matter. Much of it, like St.
Christopher, exists beyond these confines. My son Christopher is big and dark-haired and would gladly, if called
upon, take up the task of his namesake.

My third son is Rory, twelve, who was named for Rory
O'Connor, the last ard-ri or high king of Ireland. Rory
O'Connor resigned his kingship and retired to a monastery,
but the act was not as pious as it seems, for he was sur-

rounded by enemies, most of them Normans, and the title
of high king in such circumstances had little substance to
it. Yet perhaps you will agree that it was a very Irish thing
to go from king to monk, and I thought the act worthy of
remembrance and so named my son for him. Kings do not
do such things these days, nor Presidents either, and the
conclusion to be reached is that in our times the material
world is held more important than the world to come.
Judge for yourself whether this is wisdom.

My fourth son, Cormac, ten, was also named for an
Irish king—Cormac MacCarthy, who built a jewel of a
chapel on the Rock of Cashel in Tipperary around 1134.
It is in "Irish Romanesque" style, and was the wonder of
Ireland when it was erected, and widely copied. The master
masons who designed it were, however, probably from
Germany and England, and the "copies" made entirely by
Irish masons departed charmingly from the original. The
Irish had then, and still have, a love of intricacy of design
to the extent of ignoring and then forgetting function. So
you will find in old churches about Ireland carved gables
which serve no purpose but decoration, and pillars whose
capitals have gone in a mass of whorls and flowers so that
the pillar does no supporting.

My Irish adventure was to consist of a journey up the
Shannon River to as close to its source as might be contrived afloat. Then I would, returning, go to Dublin by
that one canal, the Grand Canal, which still links the
Shannon and the capital of Ireland. One other besides my
sons was to accompany us on this voyage, Mr. Thomas
O'Keeffe, who teaches at Bishop Montgomery High School
in Torrance, California, and returns to his native Ireland
each summer.

It was Tom who had assured me that there was a canal
still open linking the Shannon and Dublin, and it was he
who hired the vast powerboat at Garrykennedy on Lough
Derg in which we would make our voyage. He had no

experience of boats or of navigation, but being Irish he did not need any, for I have found of my countrymen that they are capable of anything at all, provided the filling out of a lot of forms and the observance of a shoal of bylaws is not involved.

When at the end of the school year, Tom went back to Ireland, I asked him to hire a boat for eight passengers. When I was ready to depart for Ireland myself, not having heard from him, I cabled asking whether the boat was available. His reply was: "HAVE ONE MORE BOAT THAN THE IRISH NAVY"—the Irish Navy having but that week disposed of its last vessel, the Viking menace having been dispelled by Brian Boru on the field of Clontarf in 1014, and the English peaceably disposed at last.

So all was ready, and we set out, my sons and I, for our adventure.

You are aware, I am sure, that travelers with appointments meet each other at the right place and time only by consent of the stars, or by other occult influences, and no human calculations based on timetables and methods of travel are of any avail. The stars were ill-disposed in my case. My meeting with my sons in Ireland wound up in an enormous hash with me and my smallest son, Cormac (who will hereafter be called Coco), in Limerick, Christopher and Rory in Chicago, and Kevin in either Amsterdam or London. To a degree this confusion resulted from the introduction on transatlantic routes of larger airplanes, for there seems to be a rule of flying which goes as follows: the punctuality of airlines is in inverse proportion to the size of the planes they employ.

The arrangement was that I was to leave California first with Coco, and Christopher and Rory would follow the next day. We all had to fly to Chicago, there to pick up the Aer Lingus plane (a smaller one) to Ireland. My super plane to Chicago was so late in arriving there that my luggage never got off it in time to catch the plane to

Ireland. Christopher's big plane to Chicago was so late that the plane to Ireland had taken off before he arrived, although there should have been a full hour of leisure for him in Chicago.

Arriving first in Ireland then, I was missing all of my luggage and three of my sons, but was faithfully met by Tom O'Keeffe. I assure you that I would in any other country in the world have been fretful and worried, hustling from place to place to try to sort out the tangle. But there is a kind of elixir in the air of Ireland which dissolves anxiety and I really believe that the Irish are the least anxious people in the world. There is no secret either to this absence of anxiety on their part. It lies in the realization that man lives in eternity, and time therefore is an illusion which is not to be taken seriously. There is no one in Ireland in my experience who attaches any importance to time, while everyone, I believe, has a strong sense of eternity. Time and eternity are, of course, the opposites of each other, so if you believe in the one you cannot take the other seriously. Not taking time seriously dissolves the greater portion of frets and worries in this world. I recommend the attitude if you are harassed in your daily life.

The soothing Irish mildness, unconcerned with mere time, consoled me for my misplaced luggage and for the non-appearance of my sons. It was gently indicated to me that what was making me unhappy was the time element. If I threw the time element out, did not, in short, appoint a particular time for the arrival of my sons and my baggage, all would be well.

That's exactly how matters worked out. The luggage, freed of a time schedule, arrived the next day. Christopher and Rory, likewise freed, arrived the day afterward. And while, still dominated by the illusion of time, I was studying plane arrivals from London, a voice behind me said, "Hi, Dad," and there was Kevin, tall and strong, but a lot thinner from his wanderings in Europe. The hug we gave each other was shared by all around, for between fathers and sons, handshakes are not good enough at all.

So we were all together and if I had had any wisdom at all, I would at that moment have taken off my wristwatch and given it to the nearest small boy as a toy. But I had not yet disassociated myself from the great illusion of time, which is the slave driver of mankind, and kept the watch and all the discontents attendant on it.

Chapter 2

Tom had borrowed a car from his brother to collect us all at Shannon Airport, cars for hire being at the time impossible to obtain. He was to get it back that afternoon in time for his brother to go to the races.

"He's a bank teller," said Tom. "But all the banks in Ireland have been on strike since spring, and the bookmakers will give you two to one that they'll remain on strike until Christmas."

"What do you do about cashing a check then?" I asked.

"Well, almost anyone will cash it. It's just that the banks are shut," said Tom.

I received this information in numbed silence, for if there is one piece of paper in the United States which is regarded with deep distrust it is a personal check. I also congratulated myself that I had brought my own funds in the form of traveler's checks.

"What time must you have the car back by?" I asked.

"We'll stop in Limerick and take a look around," said Tom, ignoring my reference to the great illusion. "There's a good bookstore and we could take a look at the castle and the Treaty stone. Were you ever in Killaloe?"

I was never in Killaloe.

"Well, we will go to Killaloe. There's a thing there you ought to see."

Well, I said to myself, your brother is not going to have much time at the races, but maybe you're doing him

a favor. The only horse I ever bet on at the races led the
field but fell dead of a ruptured spleen at the last jump.
So maybe you are doing a horse a favor as well.

There was indeed a good bookstore in Limerick. In fact
there must be half a dozen of them all within a few blocks
of each other—the kind that have masses of books of every
sort and a lovely, quiet, slightly musty Edwardian air to
them. I wanted a book on Irish birds and another on Irish
plants so I could instruct myself a little while voyaging up
the Shannon River, and I had a bad time getting to the
section where these books were kept because of the treas-
ures lying around.

"Have you a fairly simple book on Irish birds?" I asked
the assistant.

"We've a ton of them," said the girl. "This young lady
will help you for I am off to Mass myself." And off she
went for her appointment with eternity, leaving me still
fumbling about in the illusion of time and material things.

I got a book on birds which was excellent and a book
on plants which looked formidable, having so many classifications all stiffly laced together with Latin and being
stuffed with descriptions which for me were almost meaningless. Pedantic, I thought the book, and rather precious
in its show of learning. And yet, when I examined it more
closely, it proved a real delight, having, for instance, an
index of plant names in Latin, English and Irish. Ventur-
ing into botany I could also improve my grasp of other
languages and learn, for instance, that the "sow thistle"
of England is the *bainne muice* ("pig's milk") of Ireland
and the *sonchus* of Rome—my Latin dictionary gives no
translation of the word.

The Irish, I have to admit, however, are given to pedanti-
cism in learning, but I think that this is not really a desire
to impress but a love of intricacy and also of accuracy,
which is a basic characteristic of the Celts. It makes them
great lawyers, for example, and the most adroit of politi-

cians, and I would venture to assert that there is a connection between the intricacy of design in the illuminated
manuscripts of Ireland (the Book of Kells, for example,
or the Yellow Book of Lecan) and the predominance of
the Irish in the politics of both Britain and the United
States. The Irish will not have it that simplicity is the best,
for in simplicity they will find delightful contradictions.
It was an Irish man, Johannes Eriugena, who in the ninth
century gave a learned discourse on the four varieties of
nothing. And it is a matter of surprise to me that so learned
a man should have fallen into so grave an error, for there
are five varieties of nothing, the last variety being the
greater part of the contents of our daily newspapers.

Limerick, of course, immediately brings to mind the five-
lined verse of the same name, rhyming a-a-b-b-a and show-
ing a pronounced dactylic meter. Nobody knows for sure
the origin of the verse form, or how it got the name of
an Irish city, but I will give you two stories, one of them
semiofficial, since it is the theory advanced by Langford
Reed, the historian of the limerick. The other I made up
myself. Take your choice between them, bearing in mind
that fact has led us into error far more often than fancy.

The semiofficial story is this. After the fall of Limerick
in the war against William of Orange, which ended in the
south of Ireland in 1691 and continues in the British Ireland to this day (it is surely the longest war in history), a
treaty was concluded with the Irish garrison, under Patrick
Sarsfield, who surrendered the town. Under the treaty,
rights of property and of freedom of worship were granted
to the Irish, and they were also given the right to enlist
and serve in foreign armies.

Sarsfield and his soldiers went immediately to France,
where they formed the Irish Brigade, serving the French
king and having another lick at the English whenever a
chance was offered.

The terms of the treaty were, alas, broken on the English

side, whence Limerick is known as the City of the Broken Treaty. A big stone marks the place where the treaty was ratified, and that is broken too.

The Irish, however, continued to migrate to the armies of the Continent and before the Irish Brigade of the French Army was finally dissolved during the French Revolution, something like a million Irish, it is said, had served in the French Army alone.

This migration between France and Ireland brought into Ireland many French words and usages. Thus, the Irish word *gossoon*, meaning boy, is only a corruption of the French word *garçon*. Among the forms so imported was a queer little French verse consisting of five lines of which the first and the last lines were the same. The following, familiar as a nursery rhyme in English, is an example:

> Digerie, digerie, doge,
> La souris ascende l'horloge;
> L'horloge frappe
> La souris s' échappe,
> Digerie, digerie, doge.

Irish veterans of France, whose headquarters were in the city of Limerick, improved on this simple form with barracks room wit and, making the last line something other than a mirror of the first, produced the modern limerick. That is Langford Reed's story, and not bad either.

My own version, somewhat simple, is summed up in the verse form itself:

> A Viking while founding a city
> Cried, "By Thor, now it would be a pity
> If my name and renown
> Should depend on this town,
> Well, I'll make both a city and ditty."

The only flaw here is that I assume that the Viking's name was Limerick, but since no one has come forward to prove that it wasn't I think my theory ought to be allowed to stand. In support of it I would point out that the Vikings were great makers of verses, and every city in Ireland, as every Irish schoolboy knows, was founded by the Vikings.

Take then your own choice of the history of the verse form, and I will leave the subject by quoting one of my favorite examples, which deals aptly with the theory of predestination and its modern derivative, which holds that man is the servant of his genetic inheritance:

> Cried a pensive young scholar, "Oh damn!
> It's borne upon me that I am
> An engine that moves,
> In predestinate grooves.
> I'm not even a bus. I'm a tram."

Limerick, in common with Dublin, has an eighteenth-century air to it. Here and there you get glimpses of narrow houses crowded up against each other, like thin, tattered prisoners lined up in a yard and leaning on each other for support. In other parts the sketches of Hogarth come to mind, and there are patches of cobbled street and houses with iron railings before the front gardens, "French" windows with graceful balconies and paneled doors with fan-shaped transoms or skylights over the top of them. The careful brickwork, the width of the street to accommodate horses and coach traffic, and the windows in some of the older buildings all speak of the eighteenth century. But the giant of the city is the castle built by William de Burgo in the reign of King John (Bad King John in England, but on the whole, Good King John in Ireland). It is huge and bold and grim. It is surprising to find that large portions of the walls and towers are of brickwork, but this is mere repair done after the Dutch general, Ginkel, had battered its walls at the end of the seventeenth century.

After we had done our shopping in Limerick it was

time to move on to Garrykennedy and the power cruiser,
always bearing in mind that Tom's patient brother was
waiting for the return of the car so he could go to the
races. First, however, we had to stop at Killaloe, and there
entered a little church whose floor seemed to have sunk
century by century into the ground. It is a very old church
indeed, having been originally built, I think, in the six
hundreds by St. Dálua (Killaloe means Church of Dálua)
and another church erected on the same site in 1182, this
latter being restored again in 1887. Inside was a granite
plinth with an inscription carved on it in both runic and
ogham characters. Now runic writing (the earliest form
of Germanic writing) is very rare in Ireland. There are
only three other examples in the country, two on stones
and one on a piece of bronze. Runic and ogham are found
together, I think, only on this one stone. The runic characters have been translated by the late Professor R. A.
MacAlister of Dublin University as, "Thorgrim carved this
cross." The ogham characters say, "A blessing on Thorgrim
[or Torogrim]."

Who was Thorgrim?

The stone was part of a huge cross of granite dating
from possibly 1000 A.D. Thorgrim was very probably a
Viking who in his old age was converted to Christianity
and, repenting the slaughter of Christian monks and priests,
erected the cross he refers to in the hope of saving his
soul.

The cross was torn down, perhaps in the Cromwellian
invasion, and broken up. Only the base was found and that
because it was used as a block of stone in a wall surrounding the old church. But Thorgrim, anxious for salvation,
cried out, as it were, from the wall, and somebody noticed
the runic and ogham characters and, in answer to his cry,
the stone was removed from the wall and put inside the
church. Should you be in Killaloe and see it, of your
mercy say a prayer for him.

I would have liked to stay a little longer in Killaloe
myself, where the great Brian Boru ("Brian of the Cattle
Tax") had his castle of Kincora; but remembering Tom's
brother and the races, we went on to Garrykennedy on a
road that swooped and swerved around Lough Derg and
finally plunged down a long hill to a tiny harbor, marked
by a ruined tower.

There at the dock was a large motorboat with a cabin
top that seemed to stretch from the bow to the stern.

"That's her," said Tom. "We can put the bicycles up
on the roof."

Chapter 3

The cruiser was the *Lady Catherine*. She was a trifle over thirty-four feet long and about ten feet wide. She had no cockpit, the cabin extending almost to the transom and bearing tribute in this to the rainy weather of Ireland. The cabin was built out almost to her sides, leaving just a little walkway on which to go forward and handle lines. She had a four-cycle diesel engine, turning a "twenty square" propeller (that is to say a propeller with a circumference of twenty inches which, in one revolution, would travel laterally through twenty inches of water), ample water and fuel tanks, pressurized faucets, a four-burner butane stove in the galley, a stainless-steel sink, and carpeting over her floors (cabin sole if you insist on being nautical) and could sleep six. She had a mass of the thickest, densest blankets I have ever wrapped around myself on a chilly night, and she had something that in all my years of fumbling around in boats, I have never encountered before—an abundant supply of running hot water.

That hot water deserves a paragraph to itself. It was heated by the engine, and when the engine had run for twenty minutes, there it was, steaming hot, pouring out of the faucets on demand and in generous amounts. If you have ever tried to wash greasy dishes in cold water, even with the aid of detergents, you will know immediately what a boon hot water is. Of course, it is possible to heat water for dishwashing on a stove, but doing so is a con-

founded nuisance, the supply is never adequate, and in foul
weather stoves, even gimbaled stoves, will not behave
themselves.

Whatever the faults of the *Lady Catherine*—and she had
some—I forgave them all because of her hot water. That
supreme virtue, like charity, covered all her sins.

Mr. Matt Ryan, owner of Garrykennedy Cruisers, from
whom I got the *Lady Catherine*, gave me an indoctrina-
tion course in taking care of her. I have the advantage of
some boat experience, and although all my cruising has
been under sail, the boats I had owned had all had inboard
auxiliary engines, one of them a four-cylinder diesel of the
same type as that of the *Lady Catherine*. Memories of
trouble with that particular engine, or rather with the gearbox, raised a few doubts while Mr. Ryan was instructing
me, but I brushed them aside.

I inquired the location of the bilge pumps, the location
of the through-hull fittings, and so on, listened to the in-
structions on checking gearbox and engine-oil levels, on
filling the fuel and water tanks and asked for a compass.
Mr. Ryan wasn't too happy about the compass. Compasses
in his experience of boat renting got a lot of people into
trouble, and he said all I had to do was to watch the buoys
marking the channel, keep the red buoys to port and the
black buoys to starboard going upriver (the reverse on the
way down) and all would be well.

But I don't like to steer from buoy to buoy (sometimes
you can't see them, anyway) but prefer to lay down a
compass course, and Mr. Ryan said he would install a
compass, and so he did. He also, almost apologetically,
asked that in approaching shore I put a man forward on the
bow to call out the depth of water, use a boathook to fend
me off, and not enter harbors at full bore, and particularly,
asked me not to slam the gearshift from forward into reverse in an emergency.

To all this I listened with reverence and attention, sym-

pathizing with him in the delicate matter of renting boats.
It is a curious truth that people will rent a powerboat for
a cruising holiday without ever pausing to consider that
they do not know how to run one. They think running a
boat is like driving a car, but a moment's thought will
show how appalling an error that is. A car has brakes, and
what do you do for brakes on a boat? You put her in
reverse, but you don't slam the gearshift from forward
into reverse, because you may take the gearbox out or burn
up the clutch. In any case a propeller put into reverse
takes quite a while before it slows the forward motion of
a boat of even moderate weight. Again boats differ from
cars in that you cannot step out of them and just leave
them sit. You have to anchor a boat, and when you do so
you have to be sure the anchor is holding, and figure
whether, if the wind changes, the boat will slew around
and hit the boat next to you (which is perhaps anchored
fore and aft) or thump into a concrete pier.

Actually operating a powerboat is more like flying an
airplane than driving a car. There really is nothing you
could call a brake on either craft, and you have to be
careful about stepping out. Just as planes run out of air and
hit mountaintops, so boats run out of water and hit rocks
and reefs. And just as an airplane is not in serious trouble
so long as it is surrounded by air, so a boat is not in trouble
when it is surrounded by water. It's that collision with land
that wrecks both of them.

Mr. Ryan's instruction over, a test of my own seamanship was provided immediately by the size of the harbor
in which the *Lady Catherine* lay. It was the tiniest place,
the walls being of that gray limestone which is the foundation of Ireland, and lining the walls were other powerboats
of smaller size, chartered to very serious Germans much
concerned with their dignity.

The *Lady Catherine* was also tied to the wall, but with
her stern to the harbor mouth. She had, then, to be turned

around, and there was only just room to swing her. A minor miscalculation would have sent her crashing into one of the other powerboats, whose captains and crews came on deck when I fired up the engine and eyed me with disapproval.

I do things best when nobody is looking. Once I sailed my eighteen-ton ketch, whose engine was dead, into a bottleneck, dead-end harbor, in a dying wind, and fetched her great clumsy hull around to rest as light as a sea gull against a slip. I didn't hit a thing. It was the nicest piece of seamanship I have ever performed and nobody was looking, for it was three o'clock in the morning. On another occasion, I stuck the bowsprit of the same ketch clean through the mainmast shrouds of a fifty-foot schooner, knocked the captain's cap off, took out a channel buoy and flipped the ice-cream cone out of the hand of a small child standing nearby. It was three o'clock in the afternoon and *everybody* was looking. That was the only difference.

Being now the focus of many hostile Teutonic eyes, I expected disaster, but I had Kevin to help me. Kevin got ashore and handled the spring lines while I stayed aboard and handled the throttle and the gearshift. Kevin works calmly and well, and between the two of us we swung the *Lady Catherine* around with a good inch and three coats of paint to spare between us and the next Teutonic boat. Then everybody got on board and we set out of the harbor with nonchalance, colliding, of course, with the entrance buoy as we did so, for nothing is perfect in this world.

This was not to be the start of the great cruise, however. This was strictly a shakedown trip, to test the boat's controls and to take her to Killaloe, where there is a fine yacht harbor and a lovely hotel right by the waterside. Here we would fill up with groceries.

By the tiny harbor of Garrykennedy there is a remnant

of a Norman watchtower, nothing but one jagged corner of masonry rearing up to the sky. It is one of numerous Norman keeps, watchtowers, or what-have-you which are strewn all over Ireland and bear mute testimony to how difficult the Irish were to subdue—and still are.

The relic of the watchtower at Garrykennedy now serves only as a marker for the harbor, and I made good note of it, for against the green shores of Lough Derg, on which the harbor is situated, the entrance was hard to find. A brisk westerly was making up when we cleared the harbor, and waves no more than a foot high, yet cresting along their tops, slapped into the bluff sides of the *Lady Catherine*. She took no immediate notice of them, but later moving along the troughs developed a roll out of all proportion to the sea that was running. The trick was to angle her across the waves and cut the throttle. Even so she was inclined to fuss about the waves, and it was plain that she much preferred calm water through which she could glide, throwing off a graceful bow wave on either side.

Powerboats are, of course, steered from forward of amidship, there being no sails for the helmsman to watch. The steering position on the *Lady Catherine* was about ten feet from the bow, up high, and properly enclosed. Given good visibility she was not hard to handle as she threshed down the lake, pretending, I think, to be a destroyer at sea in a westerly gale. Now and again she would make a great lunge into a ridiculously small bank of green water and fling a cloud of spray all over her windshield, and I got the distinct impression that she very much hoped all the other smaller boats about were watching her.

We were traveling toward the lower end of Lough Derg, which means Red Lake or, according to other sources, Lake of the Red Eye (Lough Deirgeiro); and in this area there are many islands, not easy to distinguish from a distance since the green of the islands melts into the green of the mainland.

I had with me a sort of chart supplied by the Shell Oil Company (it is an excellent publication and indispensable for Shannon cruising), and the chart told me that round about lay Young's Island, Red Island and Holy Island, to name but three. Holy Island first emerged from the surrounding lush green, for we could see a tiny black twig sticking up like a factory chimney. I pronounced it a round tower, one of those strange, almost exclusively Irish structures whose function was for centuries a mystery. My sons had never seen a round tower so we decided to land on Holy Island and explore.

The *Lady Catherine* had a small dinghy, towed behind her on a painter, and was also equipped with a light anchor. I took her slowly to the lee of the island into quiet water and found a boat jetty jutting out from the shore. I doubted there was enough water to come alongside the jetty so we anchored and went ashore in the dinghy.

Wild iris and bullrushes grew along the shore of the tiny island with here and there a golden blossom. The water, near the shore, was as clear and as still as glass and the rounded stones on the bottom showed sharply through it. A lovely quiet descended on us in the dinghy, broken only by the dip of the oars in the water and the tiny tinkle of the drops as they fell from the blades into the lake. The wind was utterly stilled, but there was the slightest movement of lake water on the stones producing a soothing rumble of struggle. A memory stirred sharply in me at the sound, a memory of squatting on my haunches as a child, half a century before, watching these tiny waves move among the stones in glittering lines. My feet felt the chill of the water around them, and my hands were numb. . . .

"Watch out for the jetty," said Kevin, and I tumbled

headlong through fifty years back into the dinghy. A little
path led from the jetty through a copse thick with grass
and nettles toward the ruins from which Holy Island got
its name. I looked on the nettles with affection, for they
are a plant of childhood. I seem to remember being stung
every day by nettles during the summer and warned Rory
and Coco not to touch them. "But if you are stung," I said,
"you will find a dock leaf nearby. Rub that on the sting
and it won't hurt so much." I showed them a dock leaf.
Neither nettles nor dock leaves are found in my part of
California. I doubt I have seen one or the other of them
for a quarter of a century. Yet how familiar they looked,
as if it were only yesterday that they had been part of
my landscape. Even the beads of water on them seemed
familiar.

There are the remains of five churches on Holy Island,
besides the round tower already referred to and a place
called The Saint's Graveyard. All were built in the seventh
century and are therefore over twelve hundred years old.
There is also a tiny building scarcely big enough for a
man to move about in. It had once a steeply sloping roof
and low walls, and it seems to have been divided into
cubicles each just big enough to contain a man. Nobody
really knows the purpose of this tiny building.

The monastic settlement on Holy Island was started by
St. Caimin. He was a man of great tenderness and had a
brother, Guaire of the Open Hand, who was noted for his
generosity. Guaire was also a religious man and one day,
the two brothers were debating what they would do if
they were allowed to fill a church with something which
could benefit their fellowmen.

"Why," said Guaire, "I'd fill my church to the last
stone of the roof with gold, and give it all to the poor."

"There would be little benefit in that giving," said
Caimin, "for gold is soon gone."

"Then what would you do?" asked Guaire.

"I would fill my church to the last stone of the roof with the diseases of the world, so there would be less sickness to plague the people," said Caimin. And I think this is a true story for it has that twist of thought, that unexpected viewpoint (better to take away than to give) that is a mark of the Celtic mind.

I will give you one other story of these Irish holy men. There were two of them living far apart from each other in cells, their backs turned from the world and their faces to God and eternity. Now and again they would write a letter to each other with some deep thought or holy observation, but otherwise they were quite alone and saw no man and had no property.

One had in his cell a bird, a mouse and a spider. One day all three of these died. The holy man, overcome with grief, wrote to his friend lamenting their deaths. His friend wrote back rebuking him and reminding him that sorrow ever awaits those with great possessions.

Monasteries like the one on Holy Island—a number of churches, a number of cells and nearby a round tower— are plentiful in Ireland. They are an Irish version of the Egyptian wilderness hermitage of early Christian times— the hermitage that grew around a man who, forsaking the world, went off into the desert to be at peace with God. The Irish often chose islands for the sites of their hermitages, having no deserts. One oratory or tiny church would be built. The community would grow and another church would be added. And so on. There were five churches on Holy Island. And there are seven churches at Kilmacduagh in Galway. And there are six cells and two churches on tiny Skellig Michael off the Kerry coast. And so on.

The round towers are very probably an importation from Italy, for Irish monks and priests were frequent travelers to Rome. They correspond to the Italian companile, or bell tower, but no big bell was hung in them, since the casting of big bells was an impossible feat in the sixth and seventh centuries in Ireland. At the top of these round towers were usually four small windows or slots, and a monk leaned out of these, each in turn with a hand bell in his hand, and summoned the people to Mass.

This must have been a dreaded chore, for the entrance to the round tower is usually twelve or fourteen feet above the ground and has to be reached by a ladder. There were several floors inside each round tower, all tiny, of course, and each of them reached by a ladder. It meant a lot of ladder-climbing before the top was achieved. The round tower on Holy Island is missing its conical top, but it is still eighty feet high. At the time of the Danish invasions, it is believed that the round towers were used by the monks as places of refuge. They were safe against fire and could scarcely be stormed since the entrances are so high off the ground. Here the monks would take the chalice and other sacred vessels of the Mass and pray and wait without resistance while the Vikings sacked the countryside. Christianity, whatever else it did, enormously softened the Irish, for the ancestors of these same monks would have made mincemeat of the Vikings. Here is the boast of a warrior of pagan Ireland:

> I swear by that by which my people swear, since I took spear in my hand, I have never been without slaying a Connachtman every day and plundering by fire every night, and I have never slept without a Connachtman's head beneath my knee.

How strange that these fierce raiders, storming the coasts of Wales, of Scotland and of England should have brought back as part of their booty a slave who would tame them forever! His name was Patrick.

Chapter 4

Someday, perhaps a thousand years from now, people may be tourists among the ruins of the North American continent. Chinese, do you suppose? Or Nigerians? Or perhaps the revived Aztec or Toltec nations. Write your own fiction here. You will not be among them, whoever they are. They may well see the ruins of Grand Central Station, recently uncovered, or the Lexington Avenue Subway, or the City Hall of Los Angeles (though there are evil people who say that it is even now a ruin). And they will understand the building of these places. They were built for use, to fulfill a practical and pressing need—a material need.

How odd it is then, living in this century, to go to places like Holy Island and see there the ruins of huge works in stone which were not built to fulfill a practical and pressing material need, but to fulfill something far more important to the men of the time—a practical and pressing *spiritual* need. Doesn't that immediately and dramatically show what great changes have come over Man in a thousand years? We are no longer men of the spirit but men of matter. Our great efforts are directed, all of them, to the comfort and health of the body and not to the comfort and health of the soul. And reflecting on this, does it not strike you that this runs utterly contrary to the whole previous trend of human thought—for even the Neanderthals were concerned with a world beyond their world of ice, and buried weapons and tools with their dead.

I mention this to give you some conception of how strange it is to visit a place like Holy Island, where every stone is concerned with immortality. Holy Island? All Ireland is such a place—not quite in this world. Ireland is a kind of an anteroom to Heaven; and as soon as you reach Ireland you realize you have left the abode of modern materialistic man for ancient (oh, so ancient) spiritual man, still living on like an angel from Eden, unaware of the bustle of Times Square and Piccadilly Circus.

This emphasis on the spirit and on immortality is the very essence of Ireland, and you cannot understand Ireland or the Irish without it. It explains the character of the individual Irishman, his remarkable lack of concern regarding time and money, his ease in the world, and his essential good humor.

On Holy Island, among the tiny churches, erected with such labor for non-worldly use, the sense of the spirit is so strong that I think half an hour's quiet on the island would work enough good to carry a man through a year of New York or Chicago. Certainly I myself felt the years fall off like a dry skin and, moving among the stones, felt calmer and stronger than I had in a very long time.

We left Holy Island much subdued, and headed south-southwest down Lough Derg to Killaloe, which lies at the southern end of the lake where the Shannon, leaving, becomes once again a river. Before us, rising above the green velvet of the fields, were the Arra Mountains and beyond them, higher still, the Slievefelim range. Where the sunlight struck them the mountains were gold and purple, but in the shadows they were a deep blue. But like all the mountains of Ireland, they have an air of mystery to them, appearing and disappearing in wreaths of silver clouds as if the Druids, who once cast a silver mist over the whole of Ireland to forestall an invasion, were still at work up there.

This southern end of Lough Derg is mountainous by Irish standards. To be sure, the highest peaks are not much more than two thousand feet, yet the clarity of the air, the smallness of the houses and the fields make them seem far mightier. And if you move just a few miles westward into Connemara and County Galway, you will find the Twelve Bens, which are for me a model of what all mountains should be—grim, strong and defiant of earth and sky. They are not very high, but seem high, and are therefore enormous. Behind these peaks is the ridge of the Maumturk Mountains, leading, if my geography has not deserted me, into the Joyce country. The Joyce country was not named for James Joyce, but for a group of Welsh emigrants who settled there in the thirteenth century, being engaged in the wool trade, I think. They retained their identity long enough to give their name to the whole district. It is a wild area of rushes and rocks and fields, with the shadows of the clouds chasing each other across the faces of the mountains, and the nearest succor in the lovely little village of Leenane.

The Shannon is a river of more than ordinary significance, for it divides Ireland geographically and climatically and culturally. That's a lot for one river. It flows north and south and it is about two hundred and forty miles in length, but in all that length it falls only one hundred forty-four feet, and of that fall, one hundred feet occurs in the short distance between the end of Lough Derg and the city of Limerick. So for the greater part of its length the Shannon is a slow-moving, meandering stream, often expanding into lakes and flowing through the flat green pastureland of the central plain of Ireland.

Cutting the island in two (but not in half, for the eastern portion is by far the biggest), the Shannon pro-

vides a natural boundary; and in the innumerable attempts
made at the conquest and subjection of Ireland, the Irish
were constantly driven across the Shannon to the western
portion. Here the coastal mountains start to rise, and the
lush meadows of the central plain give way to boglands
and mountain valleys of slate and of stones. This part of
Ireland is the most Irish part and is called the Gaeltacht,
meaning roughly the Irish Place. The eastern portion, lush
and richer, in which the invaders settled, is called the
Galltacht (meaning roughly the Strangers' Place). The
two portions stare at each other across the smiling river,
and castles on one side are watched by castles on the
other. The pike in the Shannon, it is said, had many a
good drink of blood.

The climate of the Gaeltacht is rainier and windier than
that to the east of the Shannon. This produces a difference
in vegetation and that produces a difference in living.
Timber is unknown, and houses are of fieldstones. Hedges
are unknown, the fields being walled in by stones. Slate
used to be expensive, so the cottages were thatched with
rushes, and because of the fierce winds, the thatch was kept
in place by throwing a fishing net over the top when a
gale threatened, and hanging stones on the ends of the net
to keep it there.

You won't find in the western portion the big horses
and the sleek cattle for which Ireland is famous. Instead
there are sheep on every mountainside and clothing is of
wool and raincoats outside the cities are rare. The countryman knows that homespun will turn water just as well.

The roads are good, however, though narrow, and you
will find that the surface of the sea road from Spiddle to
Roundstone is green. It is metaled with chips of green
marble from a nearby quarry. The approach to town,
hamlet or village in the Gaeltacht is announced by the rich
scent of peat smoke in the air, and out on the bogs you
will find, in the great loneliness of the land, a couple of

men cutting peat (it is called turf) for their winter use. They may know as much about New York, Chicago and Philadelphia as you, having worked there some years, so don't be deceived by their country look into thinking them untraveled. I met a New York bus driver cutting peat on the road outside Clifden. The only sound about him was the clump of his *slán* and the cry of a curlew over toward the Bens.

"Do you miss the Fifth Avenue bus?" I asked.

"I do not," he said. And he added, turning to more important things, "That is a great wind we're having. It will dry the turf early. Thank God."

That last one hundred feet of fall of the Shannon, in the short distance between Lough Derg and Limerick, is but one of the river's many gifts to Ireland. It made possible the Shannon Scheme, whereby with the use of turbines the whole island is supplied with electric light and power. Ireland has no fuel other than turf, and country Ireland was lit by candles and lanterns well into the present century. "The candle that shines in the window at night" was no figment of poetic imagination, but a very practical device for helping a man find his home in the dark.

But when Ireland achieved freedom the Irish government initiated the Shannon Scheme, harnessing the one hundred foot fall of the river outside Limerick to generate electricity. The work was done by Germany, for I am sorry to say that there was no question of help from England; and a total fall of ninety-two feet was arranged at Ardnacrusha (Height of the Cross) to turn rows of massive turbines which, themselves turning generators, produce about as much electricity as is needed at the moment. How much that is I do not know, and since it would be expressed in kilowatts it would perhaps be quite meaningless for you. But the whole world can understand "enough" and that is what it produces.

Out from under the lee of Holy Island I was pleased to

find that the wind had dropped and the *Lady Catherine*, deprived of the opportunity to behave like a destroyer in a rising gale, pottered sedately across the lake in the glow of the evening.

There are plenty of moorings and slips at Killaloe, which we soon reached, and a large landing where a boat can come alongside for either diesel oil or gasoline. I needed neither, but I did need groceries and came in on this landing, but far enough ahead not to interfere with craft requiring service. This, however, was not convenient and we were with great courtesy asked to move a little to where we could spend the night in a slip, free of charge.

It was then that I discovered a peculiarity of power-boats not immediately apparent to a man whose only experience was in sailing. The peculiarity lay in this—having no keel, a powerboat does not follow its bow when the rudder is turned, but instead sideslips through the water. In turning, say, to port, the bow slips in that direction, but the stern slips to starboard. And if there isn't any room for the stern to slip to starboard, you are in trouble.

This was precisely the situation which arose in trying to cast off from that completely uncomplicated landing at Killaloe. Kevin loosed the lines and pushed the bow of the *Lady Catherine* out a trifle from the landing. I put her in gear and gave her left helm. But her stern (which I could not see) slewed around and nestled against the dock, and no matter how much helm or throttle I applied, the *Lady Catherine* remained glued to the dock and couldn't get away from it. Eventually she inched her way past the dock (we were near the end) and then her stern to my surprise slewed around and the propeller began churning up mud and gravel. I cut the engine immediately and climbed out on deck. We were aground by the stern. The skeg protecting the propeller was firmly lodged in the bed of the river in very shallow water.

So are the mighty humbled. I had sailed several times

to Hawaii from California. I had once single-handed tacked a twenty-foot sloop through a reef in the West Indies on which a sixty-foot schooner had been wrecked but moments before. And here I was aground, stern first, in a powerboat in a quiet Irish river.

The sensible thing to do was to walk off the boat and go away and pretend that I had never seen it. But there were too many people around, all of superior nautical knowledge and all pitying me, and I couldn't contrive to get away unseen.

I yelled to Kevin to push her head off, and he yelled to me to push her stern off. I decided that never had a father so idiotic a son, and he decided that never had a son so idiotic a father. And then a small man came along and said something and while we were all confusing each other the river solved the whole problem. It gently took the head of the *Lady Catherine* and turned it downstream, and the stern worked free. I jumped on board, followed by Kevin, started the engine and we crawled away. We made a big turn out in the river and came back and got into the slip, watched cautiously by all the boat owners who had just had a demonstration of what a ninny I was. That evening I tried very hard to find something I had done during this misadventure which was creditable, but everything I had done was wrong. But I had learned that peculiarity of powerboats which is that when you turn the bow to the left, the stern turns to the right. It was worth knowing.

I must be honest and say something now about the food in Ireland. You will never get better bread anywhere in the world than in Ireland, for it is largely home-baked "soda bread." Even the bakery bread is good. You will never get better eggs or better tomatoes anywhere in the world than in Ireland. If bread and eggs and tomatoes are sufficient for your diet, then Ireland is the place for you. But if you require other things then you will find Ireland, to be mild about it, disappointing. Not only are the vegetables poor, but even the canned food is second- or third-rate.

Canned beans, for instance, are small and orange-colored and so sweetened you could use them in your tea. I will pass quickly over canned meats, remarking merely that I have seen better ulcers. Cheese is good but not excellent (and cheese should be excellent; otherwise it has little to recommend it over soap). Butter is greasy. That was a great surprise to me, I assure you, and I think a recent development, for when, eight years earlier, I was in Ireland, the butter was just wonderful. An even greater surprise was the ridiculous things that were offered as potatoes. The Irish potato is famous all over the world except in Ireland, where it is infamous. It is a horrid little knob full of bad spots produced by frost or blight or worms or some kind of curse. Search as I might, I could not find decent potatoes for sale in the whole of Ireland, and in the matter of potatoes it is my firm conviction that Ireland has not yet recovered from the famine.

It is brutal of me to bring up the subject of meat, yet I must. There is basically nothing wrong with Irish meat except that there are very few butchers who know their trade in Ireland. The secret of good meat—whether pork, mutton, lamb, veal or beef—is good butchering. Meat must be hung to give it the right consistency and flavor. Meat in Ireland very often is not. I have been offered many a time a greasy hunk of a freshly killed sheep and told it was a chop; or a gobbet of green beef from some unknown part of a bullock has been confidently put before me as a sirloin roast. Perhaps in the cities matters are better. I did most of my buying in small country towns. Yet I never thought of meat in Ireland without a sinking heart and a waning appetite. We had to settle very largely for stew because steaks and roasts were not to be had. The meat we got, with some notable exceptions, was untrimmed and full of fat and bone and gristle, hacked off the joint with a hatchet and a saw. Better is certainly obtainable on any battlefield. I once counted six swipes of a blunt hatchet by a butcher in getting me a single mutton chop, and the chopping block he used was so scarred from hatchet blows that I was compelled to scrape the wood splinters off the chop before cooking it.

Ah well, food isn't everything, and that bread is really tremendous and so also is porridge, or "stirabout," which makes an excellent breakfast.

Did I mention tea? I did not. Well, there is a packaged tea in Ireland, sold very cheaply, which is superior to all the teas of the world. It produces a deep golden-brown brew and has all the presence of a good whiskey. It is the best tea I have ever drunk in my life; and if they had had that in Boston, they would never have thrown it into the harbor, I can tell you that.

Irish sugar is good and fails only in that it will not dissolve. It forms a coating on the bottom of the cup and is the devil to get off when washing up. But the bacon is excellent and if you want a great breakfast, start off with stirabout and then have bacon and eggs and tomatoes and with it a couple of slices of that good Irish bread fried in the fat from the bacon.

A breakfast like that will take a man clean through a rainy Monday with a smile.

Chapter 5

We stayed in the slip at Killaloe through the deep quiet of the Irish night. Tiny water noises, lappings and tinklings and gurglings interrupted by the harsh croak of a heron soothed me into sleep, and I slept under a ton of those thick blankets, for the boat was as cold as the underside of an eel. Basically it was cold because it had not been lived in for a day or two. Boats are like that. They need human beings and become tomblike in their absence. Later I found a gas heater which could be lit for a little while before we retired and which took the damp out of the air. But that first night I shivered and thought longingly of the rising of the sun and the warmth of day.

I was up early. Kevin lay stretched on the bunk opposite as calm and grave as a crusader on his tomb. He is bigger than I now—almost six feet. I had not seen him for four months during which time he had been on his travels in Europe. I am a chatterer and he, by nature, is quiet, so we get along very well together. He has more solid sense than I and displayed it by opening one eye, looking at me in disbelief and pulling his ton of blankets over his head. I washed in that splendid hot water, which I trust you will forgive me for mentioning again, put on a kettle for tea and stepped out on deck.

I stepped into the center of a pearl. The air and the world all about me was nacreous; silver gray and mystical. All edges had gone and trees loomed on the verge of visibility, as if waiting to come into being. The boats about were but so many crouching shapes, creatures from a place between the quick and the dead. The jetty slid off into nothingness a few feet or perhaps five thousand miles distant; it was not possible to say. Somewhere in this pearly world the unseen water tinkled and sighed and from the top of one of the pilings supporting the slips, a large gray heron examined me solemnly.

The heron stretched his wings deliberately, combed them with his bill and then folded them. He fluffed his feathers out a little, for he was cold, and began preening his breast. When his preening was done, he raised his wings and with a little hop glided off the top of the piling and into nothingness. Then a horn blew somewhere and the magic was gone, and I went below to serve breakfast to my crew.

During this first part of the voyage we had agreed that we would explore Lough Derg; and since we were now setting off in earnest, we called in, after breakfast, at Garrykennedy to get the bicycles which I have mentioned before. Tom had hired four of these in Nenagh and they were splendid steeds indeed. They were painted in scarlet and gold, and were absolutely new. He had them in a lady's backyard in Garrykennedy, and as soon as we saw them we decided we should go immediately for a ride. All in all, this was an error. Garrykennedy lies at the lakeside end of what must be one of the longest hills in Ireland. It isn't a steep hill by any means, but it is persistent.

If you are in good shape I suppose it is only two miles long, but if you are in my normal condition, which is on the slack side, that hill is interminable. I stuck to the work at the pedals until I could scarcely draw breath, and the muscles of my thighs were trembling. Then, surprised that one as young as I should actually be so old, I got off and pushed the bicycle, which had greatly increased in weight. I pushed it a little way and then rode it a little way and then pushed it again; and finally, Kevin and Christopher dutifully staying with me (they had Rory and Cormac on the back of their bicycles), we got to the top of the hill.

Then, of course, came the reward. We turned around and started down and I discovered again the pure delight of riding a bicycle, which is compounded by the little whirring noise the tires make on the road and the hum of the spokes in the air and the tugging of the wind at your clothes and hair, and the blur of the hedges flying by, and the excitement of the bumps when you hit a rough spot. All in all, shock absorbers are a mixed blessing. There is something thrilling about going over a bump without a shock absorber—at least on a bicycle. Forty minutes were spent in getting up that hill, but only ten were needed to whirl down it, and if you want to go from fifty or sixty years of age to fifteen in a hurry, get yourself a bicycle at the top of a long hill and ride it to the bottom, shouting to the flying birds.

When we got to the bottom we put the bicycles sedately on the cabintop and set out, very happy, for whatever lay ahead.

Lough Derg is the longest lake in the Shannon system, being just over twenty miles from one end to the other. The mountains at the southern end contribute to sudden squalls by funneling the wind through the gaps between them, and the lake can become very rough in a hurry. Frankly, nobody was very much worried about this in setting out, but I did suggest that we tie the bicycles down on the cabintop before getting underway. It was fortunate that we did, for we had hardly cleared the harbor before the wind came up.

It was nothing drastic, just a good twenty-mile-an-hour blow, which raised maybe two-foot waves on the surface of the lake. But the *Lady Catherine* got a little panicky and rolled in monstrous fashion, throwing over the dining-room table and flinging cushions on the floor. I could for

a while hear the four bicycles dancing a minuet on the
cabintop. Kevin and Chris tightened the lashings and we
left the cabin table where it was—upside down on the
floor. It was not fastened to the floor and that was its
trouble. But when we got used to the motion of the boat
in any kind of sea, we found that by just turning the table
a little to put its long axis along the line of the roll, it
could stay on its feet quite handily.

To cure the roll itself, it was only necessary to alter
our course so that the *Lady Catherine* ran catercorner to
the seas. This called, however, for changing course every
now and again to bring the seas on the other quarter; and
when wind and sea were directly behind her, the *Lady
Catherine* got very disturbed indeed and had to be consoled with a kind word and a touch more fuel to the
engine.

We had decided to move up the lake and find a sheltered
anchorage, and I now ran into a curious problem resulting
from the need to switch from one scale of distance meas-
urement to another—from ocean charts, with which I was
familiar, to lake charts, with which I was not. The chart
before me (it was really a map, for it showed no sounding or reefs or other features which are essential on charts)
showed a group of islands ahead, and I decided that I
would pass through them and then turn over toward the
Tipperary shore and look for our anchorage. Ridiculous
as it sounds, I could not identify the islands concerned.
The ones I could see ahead had no relationship to the
ones shown on the chart. They were small and in the
wrong position.

"Which islands are you looking for?" asked Kevin, and
I showed him.

"You passed through them already. They're behind us,"
he replied. And so I had, completely misreading the scale
of the chart. The switch from vast to small continued to
confuse me, and for a couple of days I had to consult

with Kevin and Christopher on all navigation problems.

It isn't really precious to talk about navigation problems on a lake. The rise and fall of tide are negligible, to be sure, and so is the current on Lough Derg. But there is the matter of wind, which veers around the mountains and around the ends of islands and has more effect on a boat—particularly a cruiser like the *Lady Catherine* with her big superstructure—than on the water she is floating in. And there was in our present case the matter of rocks and reefs. It is a hundred and fifty years or so since the Shannon lakes were last charted. That's not too bad, actually, because you can cruise today in the Fiji Islands using charts prepared by Bligh of the *Bounty*, and I've fetched many a cove in the Hawaiian group with the kindly aid of Captain Cook. But the Shannon charts are not available and the soundings may not be accurate as a result of the effect of the Shannon Hydroelectric Scheme. Still, a big service could be performed just by reissuing the old charts with the warning that soundings are not accurate within so many feet.

The really big navigational problem of getting around on Lough Derg and Lough Ree above is knowing where the rocks and the reefs are. You can't see through much more than a couple of feet of the reddish or brownish water of the lake, and safety lies in going very slowly in dubious places and having a man on the bow using a lead-line, if you can rig one.

To return to my problems on Lough Derg, having missed the first group of islands, I turned back and headed toward the Tipperary shore, hoping to lie quietly at anchor in Dromineer Bay. The wind was southwesterly and brisk. It was a great sailing wind. Kevin and Christopher went up forward on the bow to examine the water depth, using a long boathook. They gave me hand signals to go to the left or to the right in some of the trickier passages and I made a further discovery about powerboats—they don't steer in a crosswind with the throttle at idle. To get steerage I had to open up the throttle in jerks. This made for some acrobatics on the bow and black looks too.

According to my log, the way we got to an anchorage in Dromineer Bay from the main channel is as follows— pass a tiny island on which but one shrub is growing to starboard, standing off about a hundred yards, which brings you pretty close to a larger island which you must pass to port. Keep your heading east with the ruins of an old castle on the hill about two points off your starboard bow until you come upon a swathe of rushes about southeast with a thinning of the rushes in the center. You can go through here for it is a rule of thumb that when the tops of rushes are just breaking the surface, you have three feet of water below. Once you are through the rushes you may come in pretty close to the shore heading toward the ruins, but in this part you may find the visibility through the water is not much more than two feet, so use a boathook for sounding. Let go your hook and back up, with a man at the stern to warn you if you are backing into trouble.

The bottom here is stones and a fisherman's anchor is the best, for a plow anchor will not bury. When we got the hook down we lined up some points on the land to see if the bearings changed, which would indicate that the hook was dragging. The hook was holding all right, but we found we were not truly in the lee of the land and the wind howled and soughed about us and the boat veered on her anchor promising a restless night. If there's one thing I hate to do, it is to get up several times during the night to see if an anchor is holding.

Tom made a cup of tea and we decided to cross to the other side of the lake, where there would be more shelter and no need to worry about the anchor all night. While we drank our tea we waited for the wind to die. It would go with the sun, I knew, for that is the way of the wind, which is one of the sun's attendants, though there is a night wind that stirs about one in the morning and lasts perhaps three hours, after which all falls into a hush, await- ing majesty. The wind did die as the sun slipped west- ward, and we got up the hook and set out across the lake. I would judge the crossing at this point to be but five miles, so we were soon over.

We didn't go straight across, but passed Illanmore, which is the largest of the islands in the lake, and then nosed slowly into quiet water in a bay on the Galway side. The bullrushes grew tall in here and the bottom was of mud. We let the anchor go and as soon as it was set and the engines turned off, my whole crew—Tom, Kevin, Christopher, Rory and Coco—got into the tiny dinghy together.

"Coming, Dad?" asked Kevin.

An inch of boat and no more showed above the water. "No," I said piously. "I'll stand anchor watch." Off they went then, and I took what comfort I could from the thought that they could all swim except Tom, and among the four of them there were plenty to rescue him. It was the result of one of the thousands of miracles that occur daily in Ireland that they got ashore without mishap. And when they had done so I realized that they had contrived to so arrange matters that I would have to cook dinner.

Chapter 6

There is only one dish that I can cook with any degree of competence and that is stew. I do not know what the difference is between Irish stew and plain stew, but a man who could prepare neither once told me that the meat in Irish stew is mutton and in plain stew it is beef. If that is so, I made Irish stew, for I had some hackings off a sheep to make it with. I also had some potatoes and some of those lovely Irish tomatoes and some celery and some carrots and a handful of barley. All of these I put in together with salt and pepper and two medium-sized Spanish onions, cut up in slices. That's the great thing about a stew. You can put almost anything in it except fish and cinnamon. A young lad who was sailing back from Hawaii with me once put cinnamon in the stew and it was horrible. There is only one thing in the world that can overcome garlic and that is cinnamon, and cinnamon, left unwatched, will conquer the universe. So never put cinnamon in a stew, or sardines either. Stick to those simple rules and you can make a great dinner for hungry men.

My own stew turned out fine except that I had to skim the grease off it constantly, for the mutton was very fat. But it went down very well, helped along by some of the lovely bread that Tom's mother had made for us. When Tom came aboard, having, I think, taken a tearful farewell of his family, for in Ireland it is commonly held that the purpose of any large body of water is to drown people, he brought with him several of the greatest loaves you have ever tasted, all baked by his mother. So between Tom's loaves and my stew, we dined royally, and for dessert we had more of that great bread and jam. (*Subh* is the Irish word for jam, but do not be misled by the spelling. It is pronounced "soov." One of the principles of Gaelic spelling is that you must crowd in as many consonants as you can into a word without entirely destroying it. *Amhdhorchacht*—ten consonants to three vowels— is my favorite at the moment. It means "gloaming," and one day I may be able to pronounce it.)

I am, however, a little ahead of my story, for we did not sit down to dinner at any reasonable hour, but at about eleven o'clock at night, for the reason that at midsummer in Ireland the daylight lingers on and on and on. My sons, coming from California, were unaware of this and thought that in returning when it was getting dark, they were returning about seven in the evening. So they were in late with no adventures to relate except that Tom had stepped into the water in getting into the boat and his shoes were soaking wet and full of mud. (We found later he had a special affinity for water.) They had met a man who had thrown a little light on the potato problem. He said the potato crop was very bad that year, and we had on our plates before us the proof of that statement.

At this point our personal time clocks were still on California time, which meant that for us it was only about six in the evening though midnight in Ireland. However, we went to our bunks after doing the washing up (and blessing that lovely running hot water that Mr. Matt Ryan had provided with his fine boat) and slept under masses of those good thick blankets. It is an indication of how tired I was that I didn't once wake up to see if the anchor was dragging, though conscious of the wind whimpering and soughing around the boat.

The sun was bright and high in the sky when we woke

up, and in the sedges, black coots with their tiny chicks were hunting food. Rory and Cormac were already off in the dinghy, fishing industriously, for the lakes of the Shannon and the river itself are teeming with fish. The greatest number of these fish are roach with bright-red fins, but there are also trout and salmon, and the Shannon Hydroelectric Scheme was arranged so as not to interfere with the spawning of the salmon in the upper parts of the river.

We planned this day to go up the lake northward to Portumna (*Port omna*, the Harbor of the Oaks), where there is a Cisterian monastery and the ruins of an old castle. We had a good breakfast, and in the lovely quiet of the morning slipped away up the Galway side of the lake. But we had not gone far when we saw on the bank a Norman watchtower, or bailey, or whatever is the name of those tall, single-tower structures that dot the whole of Ireland. They are not castles because a castle is a much more elaborate structure. They are residences and garrisons for a limited number of men besieged, it would seem, by the native population. The one at Bunratty near the airport at Limerick is a beautifully restored example of what I am talking about and somewhat bigger, I fancy, than most.

But the one we saw now seemed in good shape and, wishing to explore it, I brought the *Lady Catherine* as close ashore as I dared and anchored her. The water was utterly quiet and clear—so quiet, in fact, that the rushes and sedges around the shore were perfectly mirrored in the surface of the lake, and the white stones on the bottom could be seen in every detail. A small jetty of stone—the remnant of a much older structure—led from the shore by the castle into the lake and made an excellent place to bring the dinghy alongside. In Amsterdam, Kevin had caught a cold which was now in full bloom, so he stayed aboard while the rest of us went ashore.

The castle (I use the word for lack of another) was in good repair and had recently been reroofed with slates. A number of slates lay about on the ground and a tremendous growth of ivy up the walls had been stripped off, for the whitish area of the rock which it covered showed plainly. The castle was built on a slight mound with rising land behind it and a very nice farmhouse some distance beyond. A slight depression around the structure showed where there had once been a moat, fed from the lake and now filled in. There was a door at the back, or landward, side, but it was locked. Now I am a law-abiding man in all that is not ridiculous and I would not think of forcing my way into anybody's private residence. But castles do not come under that definition. I think of castles as being part of a national heritage and therefore open to the public, and the lock on the door seemed unfair and challenging. In fact, I was trying to think of ways of circumventing the lock when a man in that dark suit that distinguishes civil servants the world over approached across the fields.

"Good day," said Tom.

"A lovely day," said the man. "We'll see no rain this day."

"Not a drop," said Tom. "Do you know anything about the old castle here?"

"It has been bought by a lady and I am to assess it," said the man.

He walked around it, we following, and tried the door, which was as hostile to him as it was to us. He noted a very large crack in the wall on the side that faced the lake. He noted the new roof and the ivy that had been cut away. I thought he was assessing the value of the castle for the owner, or maybe estimating the amount of repair needed to restore it, but I was wrong.

"Is it for the government you are assessing it?" asked Tom.

"It is," said the man. "I'm the tax assessor."

We have tax assessors in California and perhaps you have them in your part of the world. They fly past your house in a car on a dark night and charge you an extra five hundred dollars for improvement. It was sad to see them at work in Ireland, which is the last refuge of man on the face of the earth.

"Well now," said Tom, "what would you say the castle was worth in the way of taxes?"

"Nothing," said the man.

"Nothing?" cried Tom.

"Nothing at all," said the man. "Whatever is the worth of an old castle like that? It has no value whatever."

I don't want to start a rush to Ireland, but the fact is that if you own a castle in Ireland it is tax free, whereas if you own a house in the United States—well, you can finish that sentence yourself.

Having given us his astonishing assessment of the value of the castle, the tax assessor went off, and with Tom I set out for the farmhouse to find out more about the place. I met a pleasant countryman with his two little children. They were getting into a Volkswagen. (It is a sign of the remarkable prosperity of Ireland now that farm laborers drive cars and own their own houses. That wasn't the case even ten years ago.)

He told us the castle had been recently bought by a schoolteacher in Loughrea and she was fixing it up for a country home. Again I don't want to start a stampede to Ireland, but are there many countries in the world where schoolteachers can afford to buy castles? And such a castle. All right, it was only a tower really, but a huge tower, and it stood by the quiet waters of one of the loveliest lakes in Ireland, the whole of its height mirrored in the water with hawthorns and wild flowers and merry piping blackbirds all around. I won't mention the price the lady was reported to have paid but I will tell you that it was less, much less, than you or I pay for our family car. Never

mind the big crack in one wall. The countryman said it
had been there two hundred years and in the matter of
cracks, it is the new ones you have to worry about, for
the old ones will do no harm.

"You know," I said, "it would be nice to own a castle."

"There's another one on the other side of the lake," said
he. "There are plenty of them around." So it isn't to Spain
you should go for a castle, but to Ireland.

On we went to Portumna, up the placid lake which on
the Galway or Gaeltacht side is not as rough, receiving
some shelter from the prevailing westerlies and south-
westerlies. Lacking a chart, we had to have a care about
our course, watching the water ahead for shoals and rocks.
Mr. Ryan had suggested that we stick to the main channel
between the buoys, where we would have no trouble at all,
but that didn't seem half as much fun as poking about,
slowing down to examine a little island here, running into
a little bay there. And it was in this manner that we went
up the lake and saw before us, peeping through the trees,
the remnant of an abbey, or maybe a cathedral, which
marked the site of Portumna.

To the east of the town—and a good way to the east—
the Shannon comes in through avenues of thick sedges, the
channel marked by buoys. The chart gave no indication of
where we might tie up, and Kevin tumbled out of his bunk
to give me the benefit of his advice, for he had a good
head on him. We agreed we might leave the lake and go
up the river and maybe find a jetty or landing place of
some kind on the bank nearest the town. But we came
only to a bridge and a slough, giving off to the right, which
looked sheltered but was a long way across boggy ground
from the town. So we turned and left the Shannon and
came down into the lake again and headed westward to a
bay which seemed to lie due south of Portumna. Here we
could see through the glasses not one, but two jetties jut-

ting out from the shore, with a very small concrete building between them, rather like a World War I blockhouse.

"Looks like a good place," said Kevin. "Sort of a boat
harbor."

It looked good indeed but I am made nervous by harbors of which I have no chart. We came in pretty close to
the harbor, without entering it, let the hook down, and I
went in with the dinghy to test the depth of water. Chris
was with me, and the two of us used oars on both sides
of the dinghy to find out how much water there was in the
harbor. There was sufficient for the *Lady Catherine* all the
way in, and we could tie up, it seemed, alongside the
nearest jetty without trouble. So back to the boat and with
the dinghy secured on a short painter so it wouldn't wrap
around the prop if I had to back up, we went on in under
power.

It was only as I entered the area of water enclosed by
the two piers that I began to have doubts about its nature.
A yacht harbor? Then what was the diving board doing
at the end of the jetty? And how about the life buoy dis-
integrating in its rack in a very Irish manner? I was in the
middle of the area now, and put my wheel over to go to
the other jetty. And seconds later there was a horrible
grating below the hull, the whole boat seeming to rise up
slightly, and then came to a stop. I had hit a rock. I was
aground. And then the horrible truth was revealed to me—
I was shipwrecked in the middle of a swimming pool.

Christopher, standing on the bow, nearly fell into the
water when we struck, and Rory and Cormac, who were
playing a curious game of cards on one of the rear bunks,
fell off. We had struck, I knew, on the starboard side.
I put the wheel over to port and gunned the engine.
Slowly, infinitely slowly, the *Lady Catherine* started to
move. I prayed to Peter, Brendan, and all the nautical
saints for aid and she picked up a little momentum and

then, with some horrible rumblings and gratings, slid off the rock. I headed her right out of the swimming pool, calling to Kevin to take a look in the bilges and see if we were making any water.

I went out until I knew I had a couple of fathoms under me and let down the hook and took a couple of pulls on the bilge pump. The pump sucked only air. I cut the engine and listened and heard no tinkling of water entering my hull. We were not holed then and the prop had escaped damage, for it gave no eccentric jerks when revved up.

We had anchored about a hundred yards offshore. The wind was blowing strongly here, although it was quite calm inshore. The plow anchor would not hold on the stone bottom. We tried setting it half a dozen times but without luck. We moved about looking for mud or sand in which to set the anchor but found only stones. It seemed that, if we wanted to stop at Portumna, we must risk tying up at one of those jetties again. Once again I went in with the dinghy, testing the depths of water with the oars. Chris tested on one side and I on the other, and this time we poked about for rocks as well. There was six feet of water right up to the jetty, and the only hazard was a rock which lay about twelve feet to one side of it. I could come in nose first and lay alongside. Then I could either reverse when I wanted to leave or, using a line, turn the boat around at the jetty so as to have her heading out toward the lake.

Having then ascertained that I had good water up to the jetty on a course of 355° by the compass, I got the anchor up again and headed in on that bearing, my heart in my mouth, and this time came handily to the jetty without trouble. Kevin was overboard in a moment with the bow-line and Chris and Tom with the stern-line, and we had her tied up in a moment, though there was a bit of a scramble finding something to tie the lines to. Then I cut the engine

and stepped ashore. On the rock in the middle of the swimming pool, on which we had struck, a boy was standing.
The water was scarcely up to his knees, and he eyed us in
pity and wonder.

When I got ashore I reflected, and not for the first time,
that there are hazards in the navigation of small lakes un-
dreamed of by blue-water sailors.

Chapter 7

We had a chance now to use again those splendid red and gold bicycles which we were carrying on the cabintop. There were four bicycles among six of us, but Rory rode pillion on the back of Chris' bicycle and Cormac did likewise with Kevin. From this position it was possible for Rory and Cormac to reach the pedals so that there was double power for these bicycles, aiding with the extra load.

Before leaving we headed *Lady Catherine* seaward. A little drizzle started despite the assurances of the tax assessor that we would have no rain that day. The drizzle produced half a dozen children who had come down from the town for a swim. The little concrete blockhouse I found ashore was a place for dressing, and they were soon in their swimsuits, their skin as white as snow, their shoulders hunched in the drizzle and cold air, but whooping with excitement and laughter. They trooped, hunched and shivering, to the end of the jetty with the diving board and jumped, howling with delicious fear, into the chilly waters of the lake. It surprised me that they could swim, for in my boyhood in Ireland the ability to swim was only slightly less rare than the ability ot fly. When a child fell into the water it was expected to drown, and I know fishermen on the Galway coast, setting lobster and crab pots in rough waters in the smallest boats, who cannot swim a stroke. But the Red Cross has, I believe, been pushing its swimming instruction in Ireland, and here was a surprising sight—six or seven Irish children, and all of them swimmers. I locked the boat, not out of meanness but in conformity with that part of the Lord's Prayer which says, "Lead us not into temptation," and off we went.

The rain was what is called "soft" in Ireland. Each drop was but a tiny particle and you could hardly get wet in it even if you were a slice of bread. It was but the product of a passing cloud, and we were hardly on our way before the sun was out. We sped along a glittering lane with a rough stone wall on one side and a copse on the other (the trees should have been oak but they were fir) and pasture-land beyond.

I am enormously fond of hedges. The thing about a hedge is the intimacy of it, with a dozen or more kinds of plants, all growing together within the compass of a few feet. You'll find wild vetch, purple clover, sally grass, gentian, larkspur, blackberry brambles and Queen Anne's lace all flourishing in a yard or two of any decent hedge, and if you search down deeper among the long grasses, you will likely come on an elegant grasshopper, or a tiny snail with a shell as lovely as any pearl. Also in hedges you will find the nests of thrush and blackbird and hedge sparrow and even now and again the wren whose spherical home, with a facing of moss, is a wonder of construction.

There wasn't really a hedge on the road to Portumna but there was the beginning of one along the foot of that stone wall. So I got off my bicycle now and again to rest and look at the flowers in it, for it is getting to be a long time since childhood.

The biggest find, however, was not in a hedge but on a lady's fence on the outskirts to Portumna. Lining the fence, which was but a railing of wood, were two sets of the magnificent antlers of the Irish elk, the biggest of the deer to walk the face of the earth, and extinct for a hundred thousand years or so.

The antlers were green with some kind of mold, or

perhaps it was a mineral deposit. I dismounted to inspect them more closely and to inquire about them. The lady of the house said that "himself" was away, but that there were plenty of the antlers to be found and the creatures they came from lived in forests some distance off and there were many of them there to this day. So there may be, for all I know, for there are forests of the world and there are forests of the mind, and in the latter there may be whole herds of Irish elk, standing six feet tall at the shoulders and with a span across their antlers of eleven feet or so. Also perhaps there are unicorns and camelopards and griffins, so I did not correct the lady but admired the magnificent antlers and remarked on what a lovely day it was—it was raining again but all days are lovely in Ireland—and we had a little chat about one thing and another.

The potatoes, she confirmed, were bad that year, but the country was prosperous. The dianthus (there was a purple cloud of them over a little portico by the door) were especially beautiful and she wished "himself" was home so he could tell me more about the deer. Perhaps I could stop by later when he might be there? As we parted, I assured her that the United States was not wracked by civil war with soldiers shooting down students and students burning down banks from ocean to ocean. She was fearful about the state of affairs in America and so were many whom I met in Ireland. It is the fault of the press and television, which concentrate on disaster in their search for entertainment. When I got back to the United States I found people thought me very brave to have gone to Ireland, which (again according to the press and television) was in the throes of religious warfare, with Catholics and Protestants tearing each other's throats out. The only Catholic-Protestant confrontation I encountered in the Republic was the presentation of the Keys of the Catholic city of Limerick to a Protestant archbishop, and everybody was smiling.

Back to those Irish elk for a moment. They are mysterious in many ways. I have said they have been extinct in Ireland for a hundred thousand years, but nobody really knows for how long they have been extinct or whether they coexisted with man in Ireland. My uneducated guess is that they did, for the heads, particularly of the males, are often found some distance from the rest of the skeleton as if cut off as trophies. These great animals are not elk really, but related to the fallow deer and have the Linnaean classification Dama megaceros. They are not Irish either, for their fossilized bones are found all over Europe and even in Persia. But they seem to have been more numerous in Ireland than elsewhere and to have reached their greatest growth there. This suggests that when the land bridge between Ireland and Europe was severed, the elk in Ireland found ideal living conditions with few enemies and so grew to their greatest size. This is about all I know on the subject of Irish elk, except that my schoolteachers said they became extinct through catching their horns in forest thickets. A likely story suggesting (among other libels) that the elk had no more brains than the schoolteachers.

Portumna is the prettiest little town you are likely to find in a day's travel. It has, to be sure, the gray cast of all Irish towns from the use of limestone for building material. But there are dabs of flowers here and there in tubs and windowboxes, and clean streets and painted windows and doors, bright and cheerful.

The approach from the lake is past a block or so of enormous warehouses, which are a bit grim, but the grimness was relieved for me by the sight of a broken-down automobile, pulled carefully to the side of the road with a handful of grass growing out of the front-wheel suspension and an elegant fringe of grass thrusting up through the junction between the rear mudguard and the body.

Is there any place more fertile in the world than Ireland, where grass will grow, as it were, in axle grease? I looked the car over with care, speculating on how it had come to be left there. The engine was in place and seemed in good order. Sparkplugs, carburetor, coil, all were there including the fan belt and generator. The right rear tire was flat, but there seemed a little air in the others. Had the owner suffered a puncture and gone off to find aid but gone fishing instead (for Portumna is a famous fishing town) and never bothered to return for the car? Or had he just driven it to the side of the road, looked at the flat tire and decided that if he just left the car there he would never have to fix another flat tire in his life, nor worry about a dead battery or a rain-soaked distributor? I incline to the latter explanation. The Irish are eminently practical in this way and get rid of possessions which annoy them. Spiritually at least, Thoreau was an Irishman, and Walden Pond an extension of Ireland into the New England woods. I put it to you as a sensible being that more cars own people than people own cars.

A signpost in the town said that there was a muintir (community) to be seen and off we went to view it. It is what remains of a Dominican priory founded by Murchad O'Madden in 1426 on the site of an even older Cistercian abbey. It must have been a fine building, for the walls with their Gothic windows still stand though there is not the slightest trace of a roof. The place was destroyed by the ruffians of Cromwell in 1641, and the plaque erected by the Irish Tourist Board was destroyed by similar ruffians perhaps a year before our arrival. The pieces of it lay on the ground, smashed in atavistic glee, so we could learn nothing whatever about the place except what might be gleaned from the gravestones.

Some of the gravestones went back to the fifteen hundreds but burials continued long after the Cromwellian destruction and indeed into that time when the practice of Catholicism was forbidden in Ireland. There will be a few red faces perhaps at the Resurrection when cornets

and colonels of the Protestant Hanoverian armies find themselves looking straight into the eyes of seventh-century
Catholic abbots.

Having discovered what we could of the priory by ex-
ploration and guess, we set out to find the castle of the
town and on the way met a thin, elderly priest suffering
from corns and bunions to the extent that he had very
sensibly cut away part of the tops of his shoes to give him
relief.

"Father," I said, "can you tell us where the castle is?"

"Well," he said, "it isn't here anymore. It belonged to
the Clanrickardes and do you remember the Princess
Royal?"

I remembered the Princess Royal and said so.

"She was to come here one night and be entertained at
the castle and the people who owned it made a great to-do
about it and fixed the place up in grand style," said the
priest. "But the people about didn't like the idea of so much
being made of an English princess, so they burned the castle
to the ground the night before she arrived."

If that shocks you it is because one is inclined to forget
(indeed, I kept forgetting it myself) that the mild, good-
humored, patient and easygoing Irish have deep resent-
ments, nurtured through centuries of persecution, against
invaders. As his guest an Irishman will give you the shirt
off his back. As an intruder, a menace to his rights, he will
fight you to the last drop of blood in his veins. "Burning
out" is an Irish method of getting rid of people or places
which for one reason or another are offensive to the local
population. I am not an expert here and realize that I tread
upon eggshells. But more than once in discussing a particular individual foreign to the area I was met with the hint
that he might well be "burned out"—meaning his home
reduced to ashes.

Sometimes this expression was used in connection with
some of the German immigrants who have since the last

war established new homes in Ireland and, according to the Irish, are buying up all the best places in the country. (Is it not the Irish, however, who are selling them?) And once I heard it about a militant northern Protestant who, having established a home in the south of Ireland, insisted on celebrating the Battle of the Boyne (in which the Catholic Irish were defeated by the Protestant army of William of Orange) each July and flying the Union Jack over his house in the Republic. "He'll be burned out one of these days," I was told in deadly seriousness.

Many of the Irish themselves have been "burned out," and if you wish to visit the country home of Lady Gregory, where the literary great of Ireland were entertained and encouraged, where the Irish theater got so much of its inspiration and the Irish language so much of its nourishment—if you should want to visit this Irish shrine you will find that it was "burned out." It lies just outside the little village of Kinvara in Connemara (Ceannmhara—head of the sea) and when I was there all that was left of it was a couple of steps and a hearthstone. There is a magnificent avenue of beeches leading down to the site of the house and a vast beech on whose trunk Synge, Yeats and Shaw, to mention only three, carved their names. But where the house stood, there is nothing but a few stairs.

What was the reason for the burning of this splendid place? I do not know. I hope it was a good one for it was a precious part of Ireland that was burned there.

Chapter 8

The priest who told us of the "burning out" of the castle of the Clanrickardes at Portumna was on a visit from his parish in Australia. It was a quarter of a century since he had been home and his parishioners had provided the money for the trip. "Mind you," he said, "I saved the fare myself many a time but there was always something that turned up." I glanced at the shoes with the tops cut away and his black suit, which had a touch of green to it; it was so old, and I understood that sentence immediately.

"You should look at the grand new church," he said. "It is built of the stones of the castle by a young priest. He got all the stone for three hundred pounds. And could you guess where he raised the three hundred pounds and the rest of the money he needed?" There was the touch of a smile to his face, a smile of delight so that he looked like a child with a clever answer to a riddle.

"I wouldn't have the slightest idea, Father," I said.

"Ah," he replied. "He got it at racetracks. Wasn't that the great idea?"

It certainly was the great idea, for what man, collecting his winnings, wouldn't part with a shilling or two for the building of a badly needed church and the glory of God? Of course you may demur that betting is a wicked thing, and many spend at racetracks the money that is needed to feed their wives and children. That, alas, is so. But I don't think betting wicked if it is done with spare funds, for

it is exciting and pleasurable, and it is not my view that
the service of God requires us to be miserable. And I am
reminded of the dilemma of the church patriarchs when
they received for the building of the cathedral of St.
Sophia at Constantinople an enormous donation from the
wealthiest madam in the town. Could they accept funds,
however badly needed, from such a source? they wondered.
Nor could they resolve the difficulty until one of the elders
arose to address them. "We can accept this money without
the slightest scruple," he said. "For, my brothers, it was
ours in the first place."

We didn't go to see the great new church at Portumna
whose immense spire, slim and graceful, commands the
town. I felt a little sad that the young priest instead of
building a new church hadn't restored that lovely priory
and church we had just visited, but there were perhaps
many good reasons why this had not been done. Still I'm
a traditionalist and like to see the old forms and places
renewed and reused.

We found, however, a ruin of another sort in the middle of the town. It was the ruin of a substantial house
whose windows were all broken, whose front door was
gone, the whole structure leering in decay at us from
across the street. We entered it fearfully, for every violence
that could be done to a house seemed to have been visited
upon it, and I had a sense that perhaps the butchered inhabitants might lie at the head of the stairs, or be found
sprawling on the kitchen floor.

But only pathetic memories of them were to be found
in all the wreckage within—wreckage performed with de-
liberation and with glee, it seemed, at the very thought of
smashing things.

Let me attempt to reconstruct the scene. It was a gray
house of two stories or perhaps three—I do not remember.
To begin with, every window in it had been smashed and
the fragments of glass littered the floor. Books littered the

whole of the ground floor, making a terrible slippery carpet on which to walk about, and it was impossible to move without stepping on books. The books had been pulled from the shelves and flung on the floor and many had the backs ripped off them. They were good books, full of interest and of learning and they had been flung about the place by—barbarians?

There was a set of The London Encyclopedia, perhaps a hundred years old, tossed here and there, and a large folio-sized book containing a "Description of the Temple at Thetis," with steel engravings, and sets of the novels of Brontë and of Dickens and of Scott. There were volumes of the work of Shakespeare and of Milton, and of Tennyson, all flung about and ripped and trodden on by the hordes of Genghis Khan—I refuse to believe by Irishmen.

The upholstered furniture in a cozy little study had been ripped open so that the sodden flocking was mixed with sodden books, and the bookcases which had at one time had glass fronts were smashed and the legs broken on lovely mahogany chairs.

In another room nearby, there was a beautiful square rosewood piano with the keys all staggered and the strings broken by heavy blows and the real ivory of the keys ripped off and tossed aside. Real ivory is rare on piano keyboards now, as you perhaps know, and so is ebony for the semitones, but this once lovely piano had been equipped with these things and now it was all horribly despoiled.

The saddest sight, however, was the remnant of a collection of fossil shells in an upstairs room. The collection had been gotten together obviously over many, many years, with great care and with much learning and investigation, and it had been flung all over the floor by the hordes of Tamerlane—or do you suppose it was Attila the Hun who visited Portumna while the inhabitants slept?

There it was, anyway, the scholarly work of years,

strewn on the floor and the labels, scrupulously written, hopelessly separated from the shells they had identified.

I give two of the labels which I picked up from the floor. They are as follows:

Ananchytes ovatus. Chalk. White Limestone. Co. Antrim.
Orthis biforata. Lower Silurian, Caradoo. Co. Meath.

Let these names printed in this book be a monument to the decent civilized man who made his collection over many pleasant years only to have his work destroyed by ignorant savages.

Two other items in the house cried out to me for attention. One was the Confirmation card of a young girl, dated in May, 1917. I could not make out the name. Another was a message from St. Philomena.

St. Philomena recently survived the shock of having otherwise sensible princes of the Church express some doubts as to whether she ever existed. To prove that she did indeed exist (and, in fact, does still exist) she left a pamphlet about herself lying right there among that litter of books flung about the house by the Red Guard of Mao Tse-tung when they invaded Portumna. I picked it up and brought it home with me, for as the Viking Thorgrim had called out from the wall at Killaloe and been heard, so St. Philomena called out to me from the floor of that ravaged house, and I heard her and brought home her sodden and tattered testament and put it in my library. Her feast day is April 11. Remember her that day. She died a martyr.

Well, there it was, the most destroyed house I have ever seen, destroyed in wanton glee, during an invasion surely of central Ireland by the same Danes who wrecked the churches and monasteries in the eighth and ninth centuries. It is odd that not a word of this invasion appeared in the newspapers anywhere, but then, as everybody says, the newspapers don't report everything.

In Portumna we got the biggest beefsteaks I have ever seen. They were even bigger than two beefsteaks I got in Budleigh Salterton in Devon, many years ago, from a butcher who explained to me that serenity is important in the slaughter of cattle. If a steer, about to be killed, became "harassed," the butcher told me, then his muscles fill with blood and the beef is of bad color and tough. So before death, the victim must be rendered placid. This can be done with quiet talk and music—St.-Saëns' "The Swan" works wonders on filet mignon. That butcher gave me, for the equivalent of one dollar and twenty cents, two T-bone steaks weighing two and a half pounds each. But the butcher at Portumna cut me off two three-pound rib steaks for not much more, unhooking the carcass from a rail on which it hung behind him. This being a Friday we also had to buy some fish for dinner and bought smoked haddock, which proved a big mistake. Portumna is a fishing center, and on our way back to the boat we came upon a man carrying a bream weighing, I would judge, six or seven pounds which he was prepared to sell for a few shillings.

"What did you buy smoked fish for?" he said to me in surprise when I showed him the haddock.

"How was I to know that I would meet you coming up the road with a fine big bream?" I replied.

"Well," he said, "you have a point there." But he plainly still thought me the world's fool for buying smoked fish on the shores of Lough Derg.

We got the groceries aboard and found the *Lady Catherine* was a center of excitement for the little swimmers. Many is the day I myself have dreamed of boats and had only toys to play with, so we brought them aboard and showed them through and they were delighted to find seats and beds and everything just like in a house.

I think I had more pleasure than they, for often what is commonplace for us becomes exciting when seen through another's eyes, and particularly the eyes of a child. The next day, when we set out again, I took particular pleasure in sitting on a sofa in the middle of a lake. That thought would never have occurred to me but for the little children.

When the tour of Portumna was over and our purchases aboard, we got on the bikes again and set off to find a castle which we could see through the trees on the other side of the lake not far from the point where the Shannon flows into it. Rather than a castle it was again one of those square towers which abound in Ireland, and we set off happily on our beautiful bicycles, first crossing a suspension bridge over the river. Here I stopped at the bridge-keeper's house to ask if he would be working Saturday, when we would be going through, and he assured me that he would. That business settled, we went off into the lovely Irish countryside, in the soft air and golden sun.

People ask constantly about Ireland: Is it really as green as they say it is? Rory and Cormac had wanted to know the answer and now they found that Ireland is indeed as green as can be—particularly central Ireland. All about lies Ireland's greatest natural resource, which is grass. It is a resource which, unlike the minerals of the earth, will never be exhausted, for it renews itself in the greatest plenty every year. There is enough grass just growing on the sides of the road in Ireland to feed the animals of the tinker or gypsy population—who, by the way, seem to have dwindled in numbers, for I did not come on one caravan of theirs in all my present tour. The grass is thick and lush and rich in vetches and buttercups and also in shamrocks.

Not without reservations I will say a word or two at this point about shamrocks. *Seamair* (pronounced *shamer*) is the Irish word for clover, and *-og* as a suffix means *small*. Shamrock is only an anglicization of Seamrog or "little clover," and that is what shamrock is; a small variety of clover which grows close to the ground and is a creeper and is known to botany as *Trifolium dubium*. *Medicago lupulina* and also *Trifolium repens* are also called shamrock in Ireland, and the credit for this and other items of botanical information I give to that excellent book I bought in Limerick called *An Irish Flora* by D. A. Webb, Sc.D.

There is a modern tendency to scoff at that story of the great Patrick, how he explained to the people of Irish the mystery of the Holy Trinity—three leaves, one plant; three godheads, one God. No literary sources for the story can be found, it is said, earlier than the sixteenth century, so the story, some say, is but a pious fabrication of that time.

Maybe so. The fact of the matter is that the ancient Irish had a love of the triplicate and would have had no difficulty at all in accepting the mystery of the Trinity. They would have embraced it without demonstration, for the Irish from time immemorial have had a fondness for three. All they cherish comes in triplicate, as, for instance: The Three Sorrows of Story Telling, the Three Sons of Tureen and the Three Apples they had to bring back from the Garden of Hespirides, and the Three Shouts they gave as they lay dying, the Three Sons of the King of Antua and even the Three Signs of a Fop. So it goes, this Irish love of the triple, and I fancy that Patrick would have had a much harder time converting the Irish had he had to insist that there was no Trinity in the Divine nature.

However, if the tale of St. Patrick is pronounced fiction, I give you, from Lloyd Praeger's fine book, *The Way That I Went*, an earlier tale. It concerns two saints, St. Sciuthin and St. Barre of Cork (and also of Wilkes-Barre in Pennsylvania), and goes as follows:

> One day Saint Sciuthin was walking on the sea when he met Saint Barré who was in a ship. "Why do you walk on the sea?" asked Barré. "It is not the sea but a lovely plain, full of flowers and shamrocks," said St.

Sciuthin and picking a shamrock he threw it into the
boat. "Why does a ship swim on the plain?" asked St.
Sciuthin. Then St. Barré put down his hand into the
sea and took up a salmon and cast it to Sciuthin. They
then parted without another word.

This is a very Irish tale, demonstrating the dimension in
which the Irish live even to this day. The more you think
about it, the more sense it makes, for things are what we
believe them to be, and faith will move mountains.

But to get back to the point I was set on making
originally, grass is the treasure of Ireland, and it abounds
through most of the year, and is abundantly renewed
through the spring and summer and indeed into the autumn.
It is as deep green and rich as jade, and it could be cut for
hay twice or even three times a year if there was enough
sun in Ireland to make hay that many times. There were
lush meadows everywhere, inhabited by what Cormac
called "lazy cows," for the greater number of them were
lying down, eyes half closed, chewing their cuds.

Our road to the castle took us through some little copses
of hazelnut and ash and small beeches. These, however,
were made horrid by the dumping of garbage, so that a
woodland right out of *A Midsummer Night's Dream* was
carpeted by sodden cardboard boxes of Rinso and Quaker
Oats and noisome offal.

We did not, however, get to the castle. We found a
boreen ("little cattle path"—many things in Ireland are
connected with cattle), and this led us at last to a field
where we met three men returning from their work with
hayforks on their shoulders. We asked them the distance
to the castle.

"You'd drown getting there," said one. "You'd need
hip boots." He did not mean that we would have to cross
a river, but that the long grass through which we must go
to get to the castle was soaking wet. They were themselves

wearing Wellingtons, and even so their clothing was wet
from the grass.

"Why would you want to be looking at the old castle
anyway?" another asked. We explained that for people
who had not seen many, castles are a matter of interest.
The man scratched the back of his neck with the tine of
his hayfork. "I've a castle of my own on my land over
there," he said. "You could take a look at that without
getting wet."

"You own a castle?" I asked.

"Ah, there's plenty of them around," he replied. The
red and gold bicycles were of much greater interest to him.
I offered to let him ride mine, and I was beginning to
hatch a plan for the biggest real estate deal since the
Louisiana Purchase—my gold and red bicycle for his castle.
But when it came to the push he wouldn't ride it. The
castle, he said, we would find up a little road with a gate
before it. The road, finally a cart track, led through a
field, he said, and there was a big house (which was also
his but he had sold it to some people who were going to
make it into a hotel) and the castle was a little way to
the side.

It is a great joy to ride on a cart track across an undulat-
ing field on a bicycle. The little downhill rushes are splendid and the need of avoiding potholes and boulders adds
zest to the experience. We soon came to the great house—
one of those splendid manors which one associates more
with England than with Ireland.

It had fallen on bad times, but a carpenter, electrician
and plumber and their several helpers were working away
restoring it. This was obviously a house of the Protestant
ascendancy—the home of one of the English landlords
who until recently were such a big feature of Irish social
and political life. There was a tremendous entrance hall,
and a divided staircase going to the upper floors. The

drawing room lay to one side of the entrance hall and the dining room to the other and I fancy they could all three be made into one vast room for entertainment. There were servants' rooms up under the roof and there was a vast damp kitchen with a brickwork floor. On the floor were photographs—prints and negatives—of the former owner and his family, taken, I would judge, in the 1920s.

The castle, which lay but a hundred yards from the front of this great crumbling house, was the smallest of the tower types I ever saw. It was very much of a Norman-Irish watchtower and could garrison no more than a dozen men. The roof was gone and much of two of the walls. The base was smothered in ivy, which grows with delight over all the stonework it can in Ireland. But floundering through the ivy I got at last to the top of a flight of stone steps and to a breach in the wall—whether made by the weather or man I do not know—and so looked inside.

A ledge, halfway up the tower, marked the place where a floor had been. Balanced on the ledge was a white pigeon's egg.

Chapter 9

It is a custom in my family to do very little in the mornings and indeed, I myself follow the wise advice of Lord Chesterfield and will not get out of bed until quite sure that the day is well aired. We are not early starters and it was ten o'clock the following morning—a day of spangling sunshine and soft wind—before we got under way. We were now to leave Lough Derg, in which we had been since I took over the *Lady Catherine*, and head up the Shannon proper. I looked at the Shell charts and reckoned on Shannonbridge as a good place to head for, with, nearby, the little town of Banagher. We were sorry to leave Portumna, for it is a charming little town, clean and pretty and pleasant in every detail except for the damage done by the Golden Horde to the Martin house. We looked forward to visiting it again on our way back.

Rory and Cormac had now been caught by fishing fever, and we bought for them a selection of lures and hooks and line and weights which they put over the back of the boat, but without the slightest avail, for the greater part of the Shannon fish are insectivores or bottom feeders. We also bought some ice cream and "Tara" brooches and other knickknacks. The ice cream was so creamy that the children wondered just what was done with the ice cream back home to make it so poor by comparison. But it was also very soft, which is a great nuisance for a bearded man.

A series of buoys marks the entrance to the Shannon

from Lough Derg and, once in the river, the channel itself is marked by red and black "signals." I use the word *signal* after some thought, for the channel markers are various, being in some places barrels, in others pylons on rocks, and in others lengths of rail from narrow-gauge railroads, thrust into the bed of the river, at times with a diamond-shaped placard painted either red or black at the top and at times with nothing, the rail itself being painted red or black. These rails may well be part of Portumna's stolen railway. A line was built some time ago from Birr to Portumna to connect with a steamboat service on the Shannon. But the venture failed and the local people dug up the sleepers for firewood and so, piece by piece, stole the railway.

The whole length of the river has been marked in this fashion, and at very little cost. Although the variety of markers may disturb those with tidy minds, and although I have read of criticisms of the Shannon navigational aids, I must say that I found them all really very efficient.

For myself I am an admirer of the Irish talent for make-shift—this large-minded ability to get on with the job using whatever materials are at hand. I have too often suffered from official delays because things had to be done in a certain form or with specified material. I have never found this to be the case in Ireland, and the country is remarkable in that its civil servants have a genuine desire to help, and not impede, the public. It is a wonderful attitude and one to be cherished, and I will give you an example of it, which you may skip if you would prefer not to delay in voyaging up the Shannon.

One time I was living in the little village of Kinvara, to which I have already referred, and was on my way in a tiny car to Galway for the running of the Galway Plate. The whole of the west of Ireland was on the same mission, and it was my bad luck to have a flat tire in the town of

Oughterard and in a part of that town where I prevented the whole of Connemara getting to Galway in time for the first race. I could not get the car to the side of the road to let other traffic pass and soon the traffic behind me had mounted terribly while I worked at getting off the wheel. Then I found that the only jack I had would not lift the car high enough to take the wheel off. At that moment a policeman approached.

Here, I thought, comes the lecture followed by the traffic ticket followed by the fine. I was quite wrong. The policeman, seeing that the jack would not do the job, said to me, "Get the spare ready and when I lift up the back of the car, take the old wheel off and put the spare on it." He bent down and lifted the car up, and I had the wheels switched in a moment.

"Have it checked in a garage when you get to town," he said. "I may have let it down before the lug nuts were seated home."

The Shannon, where it enters Lough Derg, is a broad stream with masses of rushes growing on either side. Fishermen in rowboats, half hidden in the rushes, were hoping for roach and bream, in which the river abounds. This greatly excited Rory and Cormac, who would not be persuaded that you cannot catch bottom fish while trolling. We slowed the *Lady Catherine* when we passed these fishermen, for even at three or four knots she threw out a good bow wave and a smaller one to match off her quarters. The sun shone, the green fields expanded beyond the rushes on either side, the cows about did not even turn their heads to watch us as we went by; and seated at the wheel in all this pastoral serenity, I might have dozed off but for the antics of Christopher, who was sitting to one side of the foredeck. He was writing a letter and kept slapping at his ears, his head, his neck. Every now and then he would put his paper and pen down and slap at the whole universe. I called Rory, who was trying to catch a bream by the wrong method, and gave him the wheel.

"It steers like a car," I said. "Turn it to the left and it goes left. Turn to the right and it goes to the right. The only difference is that it doesn't go right away. So when you've turned the wheel, wait a little before you turn it some more."

"What happens if I want to back up?" asked Rory.

"If you want to back up, we've lost the boat," I said, and went forward to find out why Christopher was losing his mind.

The reason was flies. We were going through the heart of Ireland's cattle country, and where there are cows there are flies, which are the only reason cows have tails. The flies were bothering Christopher to the extent that he could not write his letter. Now I was brought up in the country before pesticides of any potency were developed. As a result flies don't bother me. If one settles on my hand or my face or neck I just leave it until it goes away. But my children were brought up in a flyless and insectless world—or in a world where insects are much reduced around human habitations. Flies really bother them, though I have to admit that hornets and bees bother them more. One hornet can scatter my whole family to the winds, whereas I don't pay much attention to them for they aren't really that dangerous.

My childhood in Ireland was punctuated with bee stings. Every summer we used to go to Merthyrville by Crosshaven outside Cork, and in the fields there were lots of those loved furry striped bumblebees which I was always trying to catch. The method is as follows: the bee having settled on a flower, throw your handkerchief over the bee and try to grab it. The odds are about seven to three that you'll get stung and the bee will escape, which makes it a sporting occasion. The pain from a bumblebee sting is, as you know, intense, and the cure for it is to run screaming into the kitchen, where your mother will get down the Reckitts Blue that she uses in the laundry and rub it on the sting and the pain will soon be gone.

With this kind of childhood, insects are of small concern to me, though they pester my family. The flies around the boat were not that bad—in fact I would hardly have noticed them. But Christopher, Kevin, Rory and Cormac, brought up in a flyless world, were harassed to distraction, while Tom and I were mildly surprised to find so much fuss made of no more than a dozen insects.

There is one kind of fly, however, that no one can tolerate, for it is worse than a bee, and that is the horsefly, or cleg. This monster settles so lightly on you that you are unaware of his presence until you feel a pain rather like being jabbed with a hot needle. Examine the injured area and you will find a tiny piece of skin removed, for the horsefly is a blood sucker. But the Lord who placed the dock close by as an antidote for the nettle did not leave us unprotected from the horsefly. It is a lethargic insect and seven at one blow would be no boast with horseflies.

The flies in the present case were not in swarms or myriads or clouds, but in twos and threes. After a while they left us and we were able to luxuriate in a countryside made complete by cows which, at shallow parts, waded into the river to cool themselves and gaze at us with mild eyes as we chugged past.

What a lovely river the Shannon is. The water was utterly quiet and smooth, so that the slightest disturbance of its surface sent out rings of delicacy and grace, speeding toward the banks. Overhead the clouds were piled in mountains of cumulus, chaste and soft as swan's-down. Now and again a darker cloud would form and, like a gardener at work, drop a little soft rain to renew the grass. Sun and shadow swept over the fields, here and

there a rabbit started up in the ferns, or a heron stood
motionless awaiting a fish. No man can look at a heron
without feeling himself ennobled. Even in flight, with its
neck arranged in a collapsed Z and its long feet trailing
out behind, the heron is a picture of grace and of dignity.
There is a song to a crane (which is the same creature, I
think, as a heron) written by an unknown Irish poet of
the seventh or eighth century. In the translation by Myles
Dillon it goes:

> My dear little crane
> In the glory of my goodly home
> I have not found so good a friend.
> Though he is a servant, he is a gentleman.

I had left Rory at the wheel while I went forward to
find out why Christopher was behaving so strangely. Rory
was making a zigzag course up and down the river, over-
correcting for each emergency which arose. I therefore
gave him the following advice concerning steering:

"When you steer a boat (or a nation) you must look
far ahead and, keeping your eyes always on a distant
object, guide the vessel toward this. As that object nears,
pick another always on the same course and always more
distant. In this way you will make a good passage. But if
you are concerned always with nearby objects, you will
become involved in endless and increasingly complicated
maneuvers, all without real effect."

As soon as he had mastered this principle, Rory was
able to steer the *Lady Catherine* up the Shannon with ease,
and Cormac too, and I, relieved of the wheel, turned to
the humbler but equally necessary task of fixing some
sandwiches.

We still had with us some of that great soda bread supplied by Tom's mother, who should be famed throughout
the world for bread making. I spent the next hour whip-
ping up about four plates of sandwiches which, divided

among my sons and Tom, did very little indeed to stay their appetites. I made sandwiches of shrimp paste of the shade of rose madder, of sardines, which were olive drab touched with a little chrome yellow, which is best hurried over, and of cheese and mustard. I also made sandwiches of plum jam, but still the call was for more, the reason being that my wife makes such tremendous sandwiches on demand that nobody in the world can compete with her. She makes them of beef patties and hotdogs split down the middle and fried, and sliced tomatoes and cheese and lots of mustard. A few ancient sardines between slices of bread and butter (excellent bread, though) cannot compete with such fare.

But when I made a sandwich with a filler of plum jam, sardines and cheese, with a touch of horseradish in case anything should be thought lacking, the demand waned, and afterward Kevin, a thoughtful young man, decided he would make the sandwiches in future. Tom, by the way, being the only real Irishman on board (that is, raised in Ireland; I was only born there, leaving when seven or eight), was incapable of cooking anything—not out of lack of intelligence but out of lack of need, for in Ireland there are always women, mothers, wives, or sisters who are glad to cook for men. It is a very nice state of affairs. Tom, however, could make an excellent pot of tea.

As I have said, Tom is by profession a schoolteacher with a master's degree in English literature. Our relationship is curious. People who are experts in English literature tend to think that writers are equally expert, which is not necessarily the case at all. But I got into a discussion of Joyce with Tom over the sandwiches and wound up borrowing from Kevin a copy of *Portrait of the Artist as a Young Man*, which I read with admiration. It is as true a book about one section of Irish society as was ever written. But of all the Irish authors (and what a great list of them there is, by the way), my favorite is Goldsmith because

of his innocence and gentleness and his simplicity of style.
Goldsmith seems to have been incapable of deceit. I will
cherish all my life a picture of him, shivering in his garret
bed in London and throwing his slipper at the candle to
extinguish it, rather than get out into the cold. Good, dear
Goldsmith. If you are utterly tired of the contemporary
novel, whatever its variety, you will find delight all over
again in *The Vicar of Wakefield* and *The Deserted Village*.

Well, I made the sandwiches and had a chat about
Joyce and also about Myles na Gopaleen (try his *At Swim
Two Birds,* though copies are hard to come by) and found
that Cormac was now in charge of the *Lady Catherine,*
his freckled face a trifle worried. The river ahead split in
two, and Coco didn't know which fork to take.

So I took over the wheel from him with all the aplomb
of a master mariner—and nearly shipwrecked us again.

Chapter 10

There is a confusion of the Shannon just below Shannon-bridge, which itself is adjacent to the town of Banagher. The confusion lies in that the river seems to divide into three. This is occasioned by the fact that the Little Brosna, a tributary, joins the river almost at the point that the Shannon itself divides into two branches—one of which is a sort of canal and the other, just a vast flooded area, which, being broader, appears to the unwary navigator to be the true river—which in fact it is.

I have said some nice things about the navigational aids on the Shannon, makeshift as they are, but I missed the aids at this point and had gone well into the flooded area when the hail of a man in a boat, fishing for bream, warned me that I was headed for disaster. I put *Lady Catherine* in neutral and then in reverse and hit the accelerator. Kevin had gone forward and indicated a large lump of limestone right across my path, and another to the left. But the *Lady Catherine* slowed and stopped in time, and with great care we got her back to the fork to find that we had to go through a lock to get to the upper reaches. There was a large notice saying the lock was there, but I thought that the lock led into one of the two canals which connect the Shannon with Dublin. In short, I had not been attending to my navigation. The gates of the lock were open, and we went in. Kevin, Christopher and Tom, by climbing on the cabin roof, got ashore and made fast our lines, and Rory and Cormac followed them and found a little Irish donkey munching the rich jade-green grass that made a thick lawn around the lock.

An Irish donkey? The zoologists, of course, would not allow it, but there is an Irish donkey as there is a Spanish donkey. The Irish donkey is very small and has a dove-gray overcoat on which there is distinctly marked a dark-ish cross, the main member running down his spine and the arms down the shoulders. Zoologically, I suppose, this links him with the zebra and also with that ancestor of all horses, of which small herds, I think, are still to be found in Siberia. (There is a captive specimen in the San Diego Zoo, which is a place of delight for everyone.) The other theory (which I like much better) says that the donkey received his cross in return for carrying Christ into Jeru-salem on the first Palm Sunday.

Well, the Irish donkey, I hold, is distinct from others, small and neat and patient and not stupid but, I fancy, enormously wise. He will carry a great load and trot prettily with it, and it is not so long ago that the donkey was widely used in the west of Ireland, where he carried the turf from the bogs in two baskets slung one on each side of his back. He very rarely complains, but if the load is too much he will just collapse under it and will not get up until you take everything off.

Irish donkeys can readily carry two pre-teenagers on their backs, and I fancy three if the third is quite young and everybody sits far back. And the way to ride a donkey is not in the middle of his back as with a horse, but toward his hindquarters, for his spine is not that strong. If you sit far forward he will likely throw you off for a fool.

When I was a boy in Ireland there were many donkeys about and we thought nothing of entering a man's field and going for a ride on his donkey. But these donkeys would rarely go very far from home, nor would they move at any great pace, the saying "short and sweet as a donkey's gallop" being well known in Ireland at that time.

This was the first donkey my young sons had met outside the San Diego Zoo and they fed him handfuls of grass, which he took from them with politeness and the appearance of zest, though the stuff was lying all about him. You could see he liked children and understood them far better than their parents. He understood that the world is full of wonder and pleasure and you must relax and be at ease in it and stop trying to understand everything. So I left my two young sons to enjoy the world with the donkey and turned to Christopher and Kevin, who were helping Mr. Lynch, the lockkeeper, to close the big gates behind the *Lady Catherine* so as to fill the basin and thus float her to the higher level.

Mr. Lynch, a man in his middle years, has been lockkeeper all his life, working on this particular lock, which was operated by his father before him. All day long he opens and closes the gates and opens and closes the sluices, doing his work in an easy, gentle way and pausing now and again for a bit of gossip on the weather, the amount of the river traffic, the quality of butter these days and the price of it, and the phenomenon as it appears in Ireland (and probably in Switzerland, Sweden, Finland and other neutral nations as well) of World War II. Some English lived in Ireland during that war and a few of them seemingly were a little obnoxious with their patriotism. One such, Mr. Lynch said, got his comeuppance from an Irish farmer with whom he was discussing the war and its horrors.

"Ah, it's a bad war indeed," said the Irishman, looking straight at the patriot, "for all the half crowns are away fighting, leaving only the sixpences at home."

Tom had been absent for a while and returned now to

say that Mrs. Lynch was bedridden in the house and would be glad of a visit. So in I went to find her in a great big bed, happy and bright but incapable of movement on one side from a stroke.

"It came on me in the night five years ago," she said. "I had the feeling of being unable to move and when I woke up one side was paralyzed." Then she added cheerfully, "I am sick all right. But I am not sick of life."

Mrs. Lynch now spends her days and nights in bed and it is only occasionally that she can get out into a wheelchair. But she had a great briskness about her and I knew I would fail entirely in my visit if I did not give her a great deal of small talk. So I gave her the details of my family and the boat and myself and where we were all from and where we were going and when we expected to be back.

"Did you notice the island in the middle of the river below the lock?" she asked.

"I did indeed," I replied.

"Well," she said, "that island is Nowhere, for it stands at the point where Tipperary and Galway and Offaly meet and it is in none of them. Many's the time himself would row me there in a boat so we could have a picnic. It's a curious thing, isn't it now, to have a picnic Nowhere. 'Where are you going?' people would say, and we'd say, 'Nowhere," and that was the truth of it."

Mrs. Lynch revised my concepts of idiom in Ireland. I had always thought of *craythur* as pure stage Irish, but she used the word several times in reference to the little donkey outside. It was the first time I had ever heard the word used in actual conversation and had held it a word used only by the pseudo-Irish. We left what magazines we had aboard for Mrs. Lynch to read and said good-bye to Mr. Lynch, who had once delighted in taking his wife for a picnic in Utopia, as Sir Thomas More would have called it. The little donkey followed us a brief way along the bank and we went on up toward Banagher.

I now found the reason for the lock. We were no longer in the river proper but in a canal which eliminated what was formerly a detour around a bend of the river. The canal connected with the river higher up. The wrong turn I had taken, though actually the old course of the river, was now abandoned because of the limestone blocks which were a hazard to boats.

Once in this cut I noticed a great drop in the efficiency of the engine. The cut was much narrower than the river had been and the *Lady Catherine* went slower. Unused to powerboats, I thought this might be from weeds wrapping themselves around our propeller. The cure for this, of course, is to put the engine momentarily in reverse when the weeds can, with luck, be thrown off. But though I did this several times the engine's efficiency was not improved. When I revved up there was a huge dip in the water to the sides of the boat and a huge frothy wave behind us but we didn't move much faster.

The explanation was interesting. Briefly, there was not enough water in the canal for the boat to go any faster. To push the boat forward the propeller had to suck large quantities of water from ahead and push it behind. But in the narrow cut, the boat was sucking water from ahead of the propeller in such volume as to make a hollow off the quarters, and producing then a partial vacuum which held the boat in its grip. Plainly then the thing to do was to slow down. When this was done the boat moved with more ease and the tremendous suction wave to the sides was much reduced.

I began to suspect now, however, that the clutch was slipping. I assured myself that it was not, for in common with the rest of humanity, I feel that bad news may go away if you do not recognize it. (It is not the ostrich which buries its head in the sand, but Man, as you have probably noticed yourself.) The engine, without anyone touching the accelerator, would rev up and then slow down; and when it slowed, the boat gained momentum, and that plainly meant a slipping clutch. Finally I admitted the clutch was slipping and told Kevin that it was slipping, for he was my first mate and counselor and adviser.

"We'll take the top off the box and tighten it up when we get a chance," I said.

"That will be a good trick with a knife and a fork," said Kevin. "There are no other tools aboard."

"I'll make a pot of tea," said Tom, which, though it did nothing for the clutch, produced instantly a sense of relief. It was a very good pot of tea and made the thought of the slipping clutch more bearable.

We were soon back in the river, entering it through a small lake, and in a very short time ahead of us lay Shannonbridge. Shannonbridge is exactly what the name implies, a bridge (of sixteen arches) across the Shannon on the road from Dublin to Galway. When you bear in mind that in the bad old days, east of the Shannon was the land of the foreigner, and west of the Shannon the "reservation," as it were, of the Irish, you will realize the importance of such a bridge, which was heavily guarded at one time with batteries of big guns. Now it is just a rather ugly stone structure, its many arches posing the problem of which arch to go through in a boat. The proper arch is in fact marked with a daub of red paint as are all such arches on the river.

We did not want to go through at this time, however, but stopped for the night and visited Banagher and Clonfert. There was a little quay below the bridge but it was a busy place and occupied, and in the Shell Guide I read of a cut on the eastern side, where the water was quiet and it would be possible to tie up. We pulled into the cut, parting the lower branches of trees and shrubs with the cabintop and our bicycles, and tied up, to our delight, to a couple of trees.

This method of mooring is a great novelty for me and more especially for Kevin. Together we have many times, in sailing, tied up to mooring buoys perhaps a quarter of a mile from shore, or set anchors in some quiet cove and then had to row ashore—Kevin doing most of the heavy work. To be able to throw a clove hitch around a tree trunk and step ashore off the boat was a delightful novelty and had for us something almost comical about it.

The cut had made a tiny island of a point of land on the river side, and it was to this islet that we were made fast. A small herd of cattle eyed us with distrust, and Rory and Coco, products of the twentieth century and urbanization, had never been very close to a cow.

"Will they hurt us?" asked Coco.

"No," said Kevin. "Come on. I'll introduce you to them." They went off together, my eldest son and two adoring small brothers, and as I got out the skillet to fix dinner, I was aware that life was beginning to pay me off for all the worries (they are not really so great) involved in raising a family.

Chapter 11

We had a very pleasant evening of it in the little cut opposite Banagher, bathed in the lovely colors of central Ireland, which are pale gold and soft blue and green and silver. The river shimmered in the declining sun and was utterly calm, though damascened here and there by changing whirls of darkness where the current moved over some boulder or ledge. Two swans with a brood of cygnets swam gracefully off the stern of the *Lady Catherine*. (They were wild swans, which are very tame in Ireland and for a good reason—the daughters of King Lir were turned into swans and doomed to fly from lake to lake in Ireland until the first Christian bell should be rung in the land, when they resumed mortal form. So no man in Ireland will hurt a swan.) There was a hayfield on the other side of the boat and the scent of the hay, some of which had already been collected into cocks, was entrancing.

I had intended to cook dinner but I put the skillet aside for a while to rest myself, body and soul, here in the deep heart of Ireland. The swans were utterly silent as they moved through the water, and across the gleaming river three or four swifts were diving over the surface, scooping up flies with gaping mouths. A fish jumped in midstream and made a "plop" that could be heard a hundred yards away. The cows cropped the grass steadily, the very satisfying sound coming to me clearly on the boat.

Rory and Coco, their introduction to the cows com-
pleted, had gone off in the dinghy, which they adored,
to fish and to my surprise they had soon caught a small
roach, which they brought back, greatly excited, to show
me. It had rust-red pectoral and ventral fins and its body
was brown and silver. It was a handsome fish and, having
been admired, it was put back, for we do not like to kill
things. Tom and Christopher and Kevin had gone off to
Banagher to get some milk and eggs. So I had the evening
to myself among the cows and the swans, and floating on
the silver river I dreamed of Camelot.

Would I sound chauvinistic if I just hinted that Arthur
was an Irishman and his knights of the Round Table were
modeled on the Fianna or companions of the great Finn?
Possibly so. Yet Arthur was a Celt beyond all doubt, and
the deeds of some of his knights find a remarkable spiritual
parallel, if that is the word, in the deeds of the Fianna.
The tale of Sir Gawain and the Green Knight comes very
close to an Irish tale of trial by beheading, and if it adds
anything to this ridiculous wisp of argument, the oldest
tales of Stonehenge insist that it was moved from Ireland
to England by the magic of Merlin.

But I had to turn from Arthur to the skillet and the
steak, for time was drifting by and dinner had to be
cooked. This was the steak of monstrous size we had
bought in Portumna, and it made an excellent meal when
all had returned.

After dinner Tom took the dinghy and rowed across the
cut and went back to Banagher for a glass of Guinness
and as much of the local gossip as he could glean. The boys
and I sat around the table and concocted a game of bridge
among us which would have horrified Culbertson and his
successors but was great fun. Bridge is the only card game
of which I can remember the rules and one or two of the
conventions. This gave me a considerable advantage because nobody else knew anything about it, but Rory

proved to have a remarkably quick mind and may be in danger of becoming a bridge player, which could cost him half his leisure in later years. A few hands and we all turned in and were fast asleep when we were awakened by an enormous splashing in the water followed by laughter and pleas for aid.

"What happened?" I shouted from my bunk.

"Tom fell in," said Kevin.

"Did you get him out?"

"Yes. He's standing on the bank. His clothes are all wet and he lost his shoes. I'm getting him a towel and some dry pajamas. He can change on the bank and come aboard."

I nestled callously back in my blankets and was just dozing off again when there came another horrendous splash.

"What happened now?" I cried.

"Tom fell in again," said Kevin, choking with mirth. "He dried himself, changed into the pajamas, stepped over the bank and missed the boat in the dark."

"You're kidding," I said.

"No," said Kevin, practically helpless with laughter. "I don't know whether we're going to be able to get him aboard. He keeps missing the boat."

"Well," I said uncharitably, "have him come on board first and change afterwards, or he'll run out of clothes."

There was some more bustling from the stern of the boat and then another mighty splash.

"I'm just not going to believe it," I said, pulling the blankets over my head. "I must be dreaming."

But this time Tom was safe and it was the dinghy which had made the splash, as Tom stepped from it into the *Lady Catherine*. It wasn't a question of Tom having stayed too long in the tavern over his gossip. It was a matter of not being used to boats, which for all their innocent looks are very tricky inventions.

Tom had rowed back across the cut without trouble, tied up the dinghy, stepped on the gunwale to get into the *Lady Catherine*. The dinghy had promptly capsized with a smirk, for this is a favorite trick of dinghies. Tom had then struggled to the bank, thoughtfully deciding not to come aboard soaking wet. His shoes came off and were lost in the mud at the bottom of the canal. Kevin then gave him a towel and some dry underwear and pajamas. When he had dried off and put these on, Tom had stepped from the bank to the *Lady Catherine* and at that moment I surmise two things happened. The turf of the bank collapsed under him and the *Lady Catherine*, inspired by a slight eddy of wind, moved away from the bank an inch or two. So he missed again and once more wound up in the canal. This time he was fished into the *Lady Catherine* and the third splash I heard was the dinghy being pushed away in the effort.

The following day was Sunday and it dawned with the problem of finding Tom a pair of shoes so we could all go to Mass. It developed that Tom's feet were two sizes larger than those of anyone on board. I gave him a pair of shoes which were terribly small for him and he carried these in his hand across the hayfield, only putting them on, to cramp his feet appallingly, when he reached the town.

Finding the church wasn't hard. The solitary street of Banagher was crowded with people, all headed in one direction, and we went then to the little gray limestone church at the end of the road. The building was new, scarcely a hundred years old, for most of the old churches in Ireland were appropriated by the Protestant sect. This has made it easier to modernize Catholic churches, and the Catholic church in tiny Banagher in its interior is a breathtaking and inspiring example of such modernization.

Despite the grimness of the exterior, the sanctuary of the church had a childlike innocence and loveliness to it.

The altar was in the form of a table so that the priest did not have his back to the congregation, and the tabernacle was a little golden door in the wall, symbolic of the Gate of Heaven. To the side and on the same wall was, I think, a "famine cross"—a crude but eloquent representation of the Crucifixion after a pattern established during the famine years in the middle of the last century. No great amount of money had been available for this church though the sanctuary was full of grace.

The pews, however, were oversized so that there was little room for the aisles. The pews also had very narrow seats. There seems to be a concept among those who design pews for Catholic churches in some parts of the world that sitting is sinful and should therefore be made painful. Or perhaps these designers are under the impression that Roman Catholics have small behinds as compared with the behinds of others. The great Father Duffy of the New York "Fighting Irish" bears witness that this is an error, for viewing once a group of soldiers bathing in a river in France in World War I, he remarked to a fellow chaplain, "When you get them naked like this, you can't tell the Catholics from the Protestants."

The Mass we attended was a Requiem Mass. A coffin of golden oak surrounded by candles lay on a table to one side in the midst of the congregation. There was no pretense that the man in the coffin was only sleeping. The lid was grimly shut and there were no massed flowers or muted chords from an electric organ. The people going past (no one missed) looked squarely at death and went out in silence.

The service over, we went back down the town and through the hayfield to the boat to get breakfast. Tom, as soon as he got out of the church, took off his shoes, which were crippling his feet, and carried them in his hand. He was viewed with reverence, people thinking he was undergoing a penance. We watched him get into the dinghy with care, and there was no accident.

After breakfast we went on up to Clonmacnoise, which, lying on a great bend of the placid river, surrounded by meadows and little hills, is surely one of the loveliest Christian relics in all the world.

Clonmacnoise is very old. I am at a disadvantage in that I do not know much of the Christian relics in Europe. I suppose that there are in Rome, aside from the catacombs, places of worship dating from the earliest Christian times, which would then exceed Clonmacnoise in antiquity, and there may be others in other countries. But Clonmacnoise is 500 years older than Westminster Abbey, for instance, and older than any Christian relic in England or, I believe, in all of Europe north and west of the Alps. It dates from 548 A.D., which was the year in which Dermot MacCerbhaill gave to St. Kieran the grant of a meadowy expanse by the Shannon as a site for a monastic foundation. The place he gave the saint was called Clonmacnoise, which means the Meadow of the Sons of Nos. Who Nos was I do not know. It was a site in the wilderness, for the land around was all marshland in those days, and so it had the loneliness that the hermit saints of Ireland were seeking. The river teemed with fish (and still does) providing food, and nearby there were the limestone deposits which were a source of stone for the many churches which comprise the foundation and which were eventually built.

There were in all eight churches, a cathedral (though of small size), two round towers and three large sculptured crosses, of which the largest, the Cross of the Scriptures, faces the west door of the cathedral. Remnants of all these are still to be found—in some cases only the foundations and a rag of a wall, and in others a wall and a doorway or window. For the sake of tidiness I will list them all, but I have to admit I had to look them up, for we found no guide at Clonmacnoise and without a guide the stranger visiting these ancient Christian ruins has difficulty arriving at any coherent account of them.

First there is St. Kieran's church, which is a little cell twelve feet long and perhaps six wide. It is without a roof but the walls slant inward, indicating that the roof was corbeled—that is, formed of stones, each one projecting a little over the edge of the one below so as to form eventually a roof. Corbeling was the special skill of Irish stoneworkers, a high art indeed since the stones were not mortared and had to be laid in such a manner that the lashing rains of Ireland could not find an entry between the crevices.

St. Kieran's church is supposed to be erected on the site of an even earlier building which was probably of wattle and daub construction. It has that childlike simplicity which is such a touching feature of early Irish churches. It is almost a toy church.

The little church of St. Kieran is the oldest at Clonmacnoise and after it comes the Dowling church, which is bigger, being all of thirty-one feet long. It is named after Edmund Dowling, who repaired it in 1689 as a place for Protestant worship. Then there is Temple Conor, which was founded in 1010 by Cathal O'Connor, King of Connaught. Of this, however, only the doorway and one small window are truly ancient, the rest being modern, and this is also a Protestant church.

To complete the list there is MacLaffey's church, which is really a seventeenth-century addition to the Dowling church; Fineen's church; the King's church, dating from the twelfth century; Kelly's church, also dating from the twelfth century; and the Nun's church, which lies a quarter of a mile to the eastward of the others and was built in the tenth century. This last is the finest ruin at Clonmacnoise, a lovely example of Irish Romanesque. The west doorway and chancel arch were built by Dervorgilla, wife

of Tiernan O'Rourke. Dervorgilla was a kind of Helen
to historic Ireland. She left her husband and went off with
Dermot MacMurrough, King of Leinster. In the fighting
that resulted, MacMurrough invited the Normans to give
him a hand, and so the Normans fell upon the Celts of
Ireland and the independence of Ireland was gone, not to
be regained until eight hundred years later. Sorrow on that
woman Dervorgilla, wife of Tiernan O'Rourke, but it is a
lovely door she put up in the Nun's church.

I have listed here only the churches at Clonmacnoise.
There are in addition to these two round towers, three
sculptured high crosses (and pieces of two others) and
over two hundred monumental slabs, some of them really
ancient, and all arranged in a lovely walk on the south side
of the settlement.

We landed at a little jetty on the river, right at the
foot of Clonmacnoise, and I think this is the best approach
to the settlement which lay on the rolling hill before us,
mute and magical. But before we reached these relics we
first passed the most shockingly ruined castle I have ever
seen in all my life. It lay to the right of us, on a small
hill, and had been blown up, but by such a quantity of
powder that pieces of it lay scattered all about—a vast
buttress here, tumbled down the side of the hill, and a
corner of a wall there, exploded back a hundred feet from
the foundations and now leaning drunkenly on the hillside.
There is something comical about it all and the mind bog-
gles at the amount of gunpowder required to effect such
devastation. One would think that an explosion of this
magnitude would be well remembered, but oddly it is
entirely forgotten, and that it took place at all is merely
conjectured from the scattered ruins.

The castle was built in 1214 at the order of John de
Grey, who was bishop of Norwich in England (this was
only a few years after the Norman invasion of Ireland)
and is believed to have been blown up by Cromwell's

Roundheads in 1650 or thereabouts. Cromwell, you will
soon find, blew up practically everything in Ireland. Clonmacnoise survived the raids of the local kings, the Danes
and the Anglo-Normans, but it was finally despoiled in
1552, a thousand years after its founding, by the English
garrison at Athlone. Much the same happened in England
at the dissolution of monasteries under Henry VIII. An
attempt was made to restore the churches later but then
Cromwell's men came through and repeated the desecration. The Irish, they say, have long memories. They haven't
really. It is just that there is so much on every hand to
forget.

It rained a great deal during our tour of Clonmacnoise
and, there being not a single building there with a roof
on it, we took shelter in the few doorways that were still
intact and in a sort of sacramental courtyard near the river,
where I think Catholic services are held, for Clonmacnoise
is still used as a cemetery. We were soon wet, yet it was
quite pleasant to hear the hiss of the rain on the stones and
the grass and see the silver Shannon disappear behind a
curtain of rain. Tom was in the worst state, for he could
not abide the tightness of my shoes and so walked about
barefoot, his naked feet as white as a bone in the soaking
grass. Rain or no rain, we visited each of the ruins and
found the grave slabs, some of them dating from the sixth
century, especially touching. "A prayer for Colman," said
one, pleading across fourteen centuries, and who could
resist such an appeal?

There were two horrors at Clonmacnoise, and I regret
I have to touch on them. McCarthy's tower—a round
tower attached to Fineen's church—could scarcely be approached because of the stench of urine. And a corner of
the tiny little church of St. Kieran had also been used as
a comfort station, for there are no restrooms anywhere in
the whole area. Since Clonmacnoise is one of the oldest
Christian relics in Europe and is visited by hundreds of

thousands from all over the world, it is unforgivable that
no lavatories are available anywhere near it. The lack
of these results in a very foul and offensive desecration.

The second horror was quite breathtaking. On leaving
Clonmacnoise to visit the little Bord Failte office at the
entrance, we passed a woman entering the grounds with
a large handbag in one hand and a heavy geologist's hammer in the other. The look on her face was not to be
misconstrued. She was going to chip off a piece of Clonmacnoise and take it home to show her friends. Without
a single guard on duty there was no one to stop her, and
the fact that she carried the hammer openly plainly indicated that she thought nothing wrong to it. On seeing her
I was seized with that sense of indignation which overtakes
the righteous and makes them thoroughly objectionable. I
was about to confront the woman and accuse her of intended sacrilege and perhaps in my indignation add some
remarks quite uncalled for, for she may very well have
been a kind and worthy person, a great comfort to her
children and to her husband. So instead of accosting her
directly I went into the Bord Failte office and told the lady
in there that someone with a geologist's hammer and a
determined look was at this moment among the sixth-
century memorial stones of Clonmacnoise. The lady left
her office immediately to follow the intruder around, keep
her in sight, and see she did not add a lump of that ancient
Christian shrine to her collection.

Before forming a judgment here, it is well to reflect
that people all over the world do this kind of thing—not
solely the Irish. They go into Westminster Abbey or the
Roman Catacombs with the intention of bringing back a
souvenir, and indeed I recall that there are pretty stiff
notices all about the Petrified Forest in Arizona warning
people not to take off chips of the stone trees and pointing
out that if everyone took just a tiny bit, there would be no
Petrified Forest for others to see in a few generations.

Ireland, with a very small budget, perhaps cannot afford guards at all her great monuments. But a large notice board giving something of the story of the place, pointing to it as both a national and a Christian heritage and asking people not to take away souvenirs and report those who do, might be just as effective as a considerable force of watchers.

I mentioned that Clonmacnoise is still used as a cemetery. The farmer whose funeral Mass we had attended at Banagher was to be buried there that day. It distresses very many people that among the relics of the great saints of Ireland should be laid the remains of undistinguished grocers, drapers and small farmers. This does not distress the Irish, however. To the Irish Catholic, religion is a living thing. It goes on—a continuum uniting this world with the next and the living with the dead. The twentieth-century farmer then is the brother of St. Kieran of the sixth century. Both are children of God and both may then be laid, in death, side by side, for the fame gained in this world is held to have no value in God's eyes. The concept that only the great should be buried in great places assumes that God also thinks the great are great. And he may not. So cemeteries are cemeteries and not museums, and grocers and farmers may be quite as great saints as hermits and abbots.

Tom, when we were finished with our tour, announced that he had to leave us for a little while. He had to get a change of clothes and he had, most of all, to get a new pair of shoes. He would hitchhike home to Nenagh, he said, and when he had shoes and clothes he would join us again, bringing more of his mother's wonderful bread.

"Where and when will you find me?" I asked.

"Oh, you'll be on the river," said Tom, who will not be pinned down to such transitory things as time and place.

"We'll wait for you at Athlone," I said, for having lived

almost all my life abroad, I have not his Irishness and its fine disregard for appointments.

"Don't worry," said Tom. "I'll ask here and there, and I'm bound to find you." And with that and a wave of his hand, he went off barefooted in the Irish rain rejoicing, I have no doubt, in the thought that there is nothing so adventurous as uncertainty—which we lesser mortals keep trying to chase out of our lives.

We went back to the boat then, and on up the gray river, lashed with the silver rain, to Athlone, and in the days ahead I came to look upon Tom as Gandolph, Tolkien's fine wizard in the Hobbit books. For he developed the same habit of appearing and disappearing at the unlikeliest times.

Chapter 12

Athlone means "The Ford of Luan" and Athenry means "The Ford of the King" and Beal Atha Cliath, which you know as Dublin, means "The Ford Mouth of the Hurdle." It is time now, I feel, for an Irish lesson, but if you do not wish to take part in it, you may skip the next few pages.

Irish is not a mysterious and isolated tongue which sprang into the world without roots. It is part of that vast group of languages known as Indo-European, and it shares a word or two with some of the languages of India. For instance the Irish word *ri*, meaning king, is a cousin at least to the Indian (Hindustani) word *rajah*, meaning about the same thing. Irish is a Celtic language, and of the Celtic tongues it is further classified as Goidelic. Celtic languages were spoken all over northwestern Europe at the time that Caesar thrust across the mountains with his legions. The Nervii and the Belgae and the other tribes and nations with whom Caesar struggled were Celts. The Celtic tongue has three main classifications—Gaulish, Goidelic (which includes Irish, Scottish and Manx—the language of the Island of Man), and Brythonic, which includes Welsh and Cornish.

There is belief among some that Irish and Scottish are different languages, and that the Irish speak "Celtic" and the Scots speak "Gaelic." Actually the languages of the two countries are so close that there is no more difference between them than there is, say, between the English spoken in England and the English spoken in America. When a Scotsman, speaking his mother tongue, wants to say "It's a cold day," he says, "Tha an la fuar." And when the Irishman want to say the same thing he says, "Ta an la fuar." (The *T* is understood to be aspirated in Irish, but in Scottish the aspiration is written out.)

Again the Irish for "house" is *tigh* and so is the Scots, and the Irish for "old" is *sean* and so is the Scots, and that brings us immediately to the ancestry of that curious word "shanty," for it is Gaelic and means "old house," though the Oxford Dictionary hilariously insists that the word was devised by French-Canadian lumbermen warbling in the forests of Canada.

Now I trust it will not surprise you to hear that the Irish and the Scots are the same people. Scot is the old word for Irish, and it is the Encylopaedia Britannica which says, "The Scots came from Ireland, a Christian land, and had brought their religion with them. . . ." So Scotland takes her name and much of her early history from Ireland, for although there were in the country at the time Picts and Britons and maybe a few Norsemen, it was the Scottish (Irish) element which triumphed. I am not going to pretend that there are no real differences between the two nations now—there are indeed. But the fact remains they come from the same racial and cultural stock and the Irish thought nothing of asking Edward Bruce, brother of the Scottish King Robert Bruce, to come and be king of Ireland. It seemed quite natural—there were also Irish present with their kinsmen at the Battle of Culloden, when Scotland made her last stand against the English and the Hanoverians. "Divide and Rule" is an old Roman precept and it has been well applied in separating Ireland from Scotland, largely by use of religion.

But we are talking about the Irish language. With a smattering of Irish (or Scots, if you prefer) you can translate many of the odd names both of Scotland and of Ireland. Take Scotland first. MacDougall is *Mac*, son; *du* (*bh*), dark; and *gall*, stranger—"The Son of the Dark Stranger." Macgillivray is *Mac*, son; *gille*, servant, though in Scots the word also means boy; *vray* (*ri*), king—so we have "Son of the King's Servant" or "Son of the King's Boy." Campbell is *Cam*, crooked, and *beal*, mouth—"Crooked Mouth."

Turning to Ireland we have Killarney, *Cill*, church; *airne*, sloe or wild plum—"Church of the Sloe." Donegal, *Dun*, fort; *gall*, stranger—"The Fort of the Stranger." Ardagh, *Ard*, high; *achadh*, field—"High Field." And the Knockmealdown Mountains, which are the delight of every schoolboy studying the geography of Ireland, breaks down into *Cnoc*, hill; *meal*, Meave, an ancient Celtic queen; *dun*, fort—"The Hill Fort of Queen Meave."

I know only a little Gaelic, but even so it is fun traveling around Ireland and Scotland trying to translate the names of places. It is surprising how much *can* be translated. And if you have also a smattering of mythology, then the countryside becomes populated by the great figures of the past; and coming to Athgowla, the Ford of the Fork, you will know immediately that it was here in the golden days of Ireland that Cuchulainn (The Hound of Culann) thrust upright in the middle of a river a limb of a tree with four branches jutting out from it, on each of them the head of a Connaught warrior, to warn the invaders what kind of champion guarded Ulster.

I mentioned earlier the importance of cattle to Ireland. Brian Boru, Ireland's great hero, means Brin of the Cattle Tax, and *boreen* means cow path. Bothar, Gaelic for *road*, means cattle way or passage, and the bardic tales, learned by heart, contain a special classification of tales concerning cattle raids of which the Tain Bó Cuailnge, or Cattle Raid of Cooley, is the most famous. A great literary treasure of Clonmacnoise is called *The Book of the Dun Cow*, ac-

knowledging that it was on vellum made from the hide of
a brown cow belonging to St. Kieran that the book was
written. This book, by the way, was the cause of several
wars and raids between the O'Connors and the O'Donnels
for its possession. Ancient Ireland and western America
have this in common—their whole economy was concerned with cattle raising. Do you suppose that stories of
cattle rustling in Texas will two thousand years from now
be as revered as the story of the Cattle Raid of Cooley,
in which Cuchulainn featured? Will Annie Oakley rate
with Queen Maeve of Erin and Billie the Kid with Fergus
MacRoy, her chief scout?

Going upstream from Clonmacnoise, we found a weir
across the Shannon at Athlone and a large lock on the
west side by which to pass the weir. The lock gates were
open as we approached, and the lock itself full of cruisers.
Many of these were manned by families from Germany
who have found in Ireland a good place for holidays, and
this invasion of Ireland is greatly benefiting the country,
which I found far more prosperous than when I last
visited it ten years ago. Many of these Germans are buying land in Ireland and some turn to farming, and it is
possible that in a few generations we shall have Irishmen
with names like Schmidt and Krauss and Albrecht. I don't
think this will greatly damage Ireland, which has shown
an enormous ability for absorption of other populations.
The stoutest champions of Ireland in recent years have not
been from the old stock of O'Connor and O'Neill and
O'Donnell, but the newer stock of Parnell and de Valera
and Pearse. It would not be surprising if among her future
champions were such names as von Eisen and Schwartz
and Braun. It is remarkable that the greatest of the Gaelic
scholars, who helped revive the language of Ireland, was
the German professor, Kuno Meyer, and one of the comic
and yet pathetic spectacles of not so long ago was that
of this gentle German speaking in Gaelic on the ancient

glories of Ireland to a crowd of Dubliners who couldn't understand a word of what he said.

We were soon through the Athlone lock and, once on the upstream side, set out to find a place to moor. There was a likely spot at a quay on the west side of the Shannon, but this was in the center of the city and likely to attract too many visitors to the boat. On the east side were some mooring buoys and we made fast to one of these. But we were now in the middle of the river and could not get the bicycles ashore to visit in Athlone. So we let go the mooring and poked about upstream looking both for a better place and a source of fuel for our diesel tanks, which I thought we ought to replenish. We found two fuel pumps on a wooden quay a little way upstream, but they had no diesel fuel. However, we learned that there was a marina nearby with the name of the Jolly Mariner, and we could certainly tie up there.

The Jolly Mariner Marina was reached through a little opening in the east riverbank which enlarged into a boat basin beyond. We got in without trouble and soon tied up. There was a bar and a restaurant and a hot shower available, and there was no charge for a berth for the *Lady Catherine*.

Chapter 13

We had berthed at the Jolly Mariner Marina in the after-noon, so there was time then to get the bicycles ashore and explore the town. We had four bicycles now between the five of us; so Rory had one to himself instead of riding pillion, and Kevin took Cormac on the back of his and instructed him how to reach forward and put his feet on the pedals so he could help with the work.

Athlone is a gray town as are all the towns of Ireland, being built, as I have said, of limestone. The same John de Grey whose castle was so thoroughly exploded at Clon-macnoise built another castle as well as a bridge over the Shannon at Athlone in 1210. The grim round walls of the castle remain, but this being a Sunday we could not get in to look about. Indeed, everything was closed down ex-cept grocery stores, but we rode about the town locating the laundry and the dairy and the post office and other places we needed to visit. The population of Athlone is somewhere between seven and eight thousand and the streets are often small and winding and, thank God, flat, for my prowess as a bicycle rider was not as yet fully developed.

Many of the shops were tiny, so small that it would seem impossible that anyone could earn a living from them. We had a need of milk and found that Athlone, in the heart of the Irish dairy country, was as empty of milk as Newcastle is of coal and Boston of fish. There was

scarcely a bottle to be had in the town, but you must bear
in mind that this was Sunday. At the first two shops not
a drop was for sale. But other sources of supply were suggested immediately, and a third place had just sold its
last bottle, and we now found ourselves part of a group
of milk seekers, traipsing about Athlone from store to
store preceded by one or two children who rather broke
the rules by running. At last an unfailing source of supply
was suggested to us. When we arrived, with all the others
also seeking milk, there was a slight contretemps. Nobody
wanted to ask for milk first—the Irish feeling that we, as
visitors, should have first chance at what might be available, and we, visitors, feeling that those who lived in the
place were certainly entitled to milk before ourselves.

Eventually Kevin, breaking the silence, diffidently asked
for milk, and the lady who owned the shop sized up the
situation and said, "Och, I have plenty of it, if you don't
mind it in cartons." Then everybody smiled because nobody had to deprive the other and there was milk for us all.

Having got milk, Kevin, Coco and Chris went ahead
down the street on their bicycles, leaving me and Rory
to come along a little more slowly. But they were soon
back, Kevin with the exciting news that he had spotted a
violin for sale in a shop window. Now I have not as many
dreams left as I had when I was a boy. I have given up
the hope, for instance, of one day feeding the glittering
peacocks of Ophir, or seeing the graceful spires of Samarkand etched against a Persian sunset—if it is in Persia that
Samarkand lay. But I still dream of one day finding a
Stradivari violin for sale in a shop window. So hearing
Kevin's news I went quickly to the tiny shop in which the
violin was displayed and examined the instrument closely
through the window.

The fact that I know very little about violins makes it
easy for me to make up my mind concerning them, for
nothing is so disastrous to decision as a wealth of knowl-

edge. This one was a Strad without a doubt, I decided on a moment's inspection. The ƒ-holes showed the sure and elegant carving of the master. The scroll could have come from no other hand but his. It was a Strad of the "long" period, which some innocent had revarnished with varnish left over from finishing an old chair. The varnish had been put on thickly and it had flowed in wrinkles here and there. Underneath this ignominious coat, however, might lie the original red-gold varnish of Cremona. A find then—a tremendous find which must be at least the equal of the Cremona violin Kevin discovered in Morocco, during his recent tour, where it was being used by a snake charmer who had mislaid his flute. This instrument had no fingerboard but it was being played nonetheless, the strings being stopped against the bare neck. It had, said Kevin, the clear, authoritative note of a Cremona, and the Latin label or ticket inside announced that it was from the hand of Nicholas Amati, son of Andreas.

This shop, alas, was shut. But in Ireland most people live over their shops and will often oblige by opening up if you knock on the door. I knocked on the door with vigor but without result. "Himself is away," said someone passing by; so there was nothing to do but return on the morrow, hoping in the meantime that nobody else would come along and buy the instrument. Before leaving I noted the other contents of the window and marveled at the diversity. Among them were a saxophone, a guitar, a mandolin, several sets of bicycle pedals, hammers, saws, erasers, pencils, plastic bucket, rolls of flypaper, picture postcards, bandages and a teapot. Having looked all these over, we went back to the boat, determined to return early the following day and examine the violin more closely.

On the following day, however, I was down with a sore throat and a temperature. It was not the rain at Clonmacnoise which had given me my sore throat but the

absence of an automatic dishwasher on board. Whenever
I am away from an automatic dishwasher, I get a strep
throat. Kevin went ashore to inquire for a doctor at the
Jolly Mariner and in a short while the prettiest doctor I
have ever seen, wearing a miniskirt, came aboard. "Where's
the sick man?" she asked, making her way through the
salon of the boat, and I panicked, immediately aware of
the disarray of my bunk, the socks lying on the floor and
the clothes tumbled on top of them. The doctor had the
grace to ignore the confusion. She had dark curly hair, blue
eyes, a pink and white complexion, very much like my
daughter Arabella's, and a highly professional but cheerful
manner.

"What is the matter?" she asked, and having been
through this before I was able to give a complete diagnosis.

"I have a strep throat," I said. "It's the result of not
having a dishwasher. If you give me a massive dose of penicillin I will recover. My temperature is a hundred and one."

"Did you take it?" she asked.

"No," I said. "It's always a hundred and one."

She took my temperature anyway and it was a hundred
and one. She examined my throat and admitted it was a
strep throat. Then she picked up the syringe and said
while filling it, "I wish I had a washing machine myself.
They're lovely things."

"They sterilize the dishes," I said. "I always get a strep
throat without one."

"They're easy on the hands too," she said. "Turn over.
This won't hurt much." I was bold enough to ask her
where she had studied medicine and she said Dublin and
jabbed the needle in. It was about a hundred and ten feet
long and how come it didn't make a hole in the bottom of
the boat I do not know. The doctor didn't practice regu-
larly, having a house to run and children to take care of.
But to oblige a friend she had taken over his practice for
a little while so he could go on holiday. She gave me a

prescription and then mused over the possibility of getting it filled since this was August Bank Holiday (the first Monday in August). Since it was possible that we couldn't get it filled she gave me a handful of pills to tide me over until Tuesday and went off.

Penicillin works wonders with me. In an hour I felt so good I got out of bed. The boys were ashore but Rory was lying in his bunk. "You're not feeling well?" I asked.

"My throat hurts," said Rory.

"Gosh, why didn't you say something while the doctor was here?"

"It didn't hurt then."

So Kevin was summoned again to call the doctor and she came in a very short while and treated Rory for strep throat too. Rather than call her back a third time, I got Kevin to confess that he had a bad cold (the same he had brought with him from Amsterdam), so she prescribed for that. She must have thought the *Lady Catherine* a plague ship, but her medicine was so good that we were all feeling fine in a little while, though Rory and I were firmly ordered to bed for the rest of the day, for that first venture out of bed on my part had not been wise.

The following day I was certainly sufficiently recovered to get on my bicycle and go to the little shop and buy my Stradivari. I took Kevin with me, for he has more sense than I. But the shop was still shut and "himself" still away. This information, gleaned from a neighbor, prompted in me a very non-Irish question for which I take the opportunity of apologizing.

"When will he be back?" I asked, forgetfully introducing the element of time.

The pale-blue eyes of my informant clouded, but she soon solved the problem readily. "He will be back sometime," she said confidently. It was an excellent answer, roundly considered. He would be back sometime, and sometime I would buy my Strad, found hanging in a shop

window among fishing reels and bicycle pumps. And sometime too I will stroke the glorious feathers of the peacocks
of Ophir.

"Go rabh maith agat," I said, but since speaking Gaelic
is a kind of social offense in Ireland, she blushed and
turned away.

August Bank Holiday is an English holiday inherited
by Ireland from the days of British rule and was designed,
by closing all banks on the first Monday in August, to give
everybody a day off. Actually, as I mentioned earlier, the
banks of Ireland were closed by a strike anyway, which
proved an enormous inconvenience for tourists but did
not seem to greatly affect the Irish themselves. This, I
think, is because the Irish are very trusting in money matters. Since I come from the area of Los Angeles, where I
have been asked for as many as two credit cards and an
independent reference before a check for merchandise
would be accepted, the Irish attitude was refreshing and
astonishing, and I cannot resist giving you two examples
of this remarkable trust extended to strangers in money
matters.

I had paid for the hire of the *Lady Catherine* with
traveler's checks. The sum involved was six hundred and
fifty dollars, and when I returned the boat to Mr. Ryan
at the end of my journey, I mentioned to him, in general
conversation, the bank strike and the sad spectacle of tourists in Dublin standing in a drizzling rain outside Cooks
Travel Service and the American Express Agency waiting
to receive funds from the United States because of it.

"Are you short of money yourself?" he asked.

"No. Not at all," I replied.

Mr. Ryan reached in the drawer of his desk and took
out my traveler's checks. "If you're short, you can have
these back," he said. "You could send me a check from
America for the boat hire when you get back home. You're

welcome to them. I wouldn't like to think of your holiday being spoiled for lack of money." And he didn't know me from Adam either. I thanked him sincerely but refused his offer, for I had no need of the money.

Again, later in my voyage, I met an old childhood friend, Fergus Cross. Fergus runs a big automobile agency and garage in Cork, and the last time we saw each other was literally ages ago—before the atomic age, for instance, and the space age, just to mention two of them. When all our personal reminiscences were out of the way I asked him how he could run a business with a bank strike going on.

"We take checks and IOUs and so on," he said. "I have a safe full of them."

"Do you cash checks for people you don't know?" I asked.

"Certainly," said Fergus. "I do it all the time."

The whole of Ireland for many months then was accepting each other's paper, which means that the whole of Ireland trusted the whole of Ireland and all the visitors as well. The bank strike was settled quite suddenly before Christmas of 1970. After all the checks and IOUs had been turned in for processing and all the paperwork was done, it was found that bad checks amounted to less than one-tenth of one percent, though opportunities for fraud in Ireland had been unlimited for many months.

It was a pity we were in Athlone on a holiday, however, for everything was shut down, and though we explored the town, we could see only the outside of things. There is much there to see, but when Tuesday came, we had spent more hours than we could afford and so had to limit ourselves to a few necessary errands before going on.

Tom returned on Tuesday, having added his own chapter to the long story of Irish pilgrimages. He had had to walk almost the full fifty miles from Clonmacnoise to

Nenagh in his bare feet because people thought he was on a pilgrimage and doing penance. He had his shoes (my shoes which would not fit him) in his hands, so being barefoot appeared voluntary. When he held up his thumb for a ride, people thought he was but suffering from a moment's lapse of resolution—a fall from grace—which in his own interests it would be better to ignore.

He was at last picked up by a priest who could tell at a glance a penitent from a mere pedestrian. He arrived home to find that his spare shoes were all so stiff he could scarcely wear them. Not a shoe shop was open in Nenagh on Sunday or on Monday either, so it was Tuesday morning before he could buy a pair of shoes and, since Tom takes a huge size, he was not easy to fit.

Before Tom arrived we had all gone into Athlone to do a few chores. The town is one of small, even tidy, privately owned shops and of small houses or big elegant ones but nothing in between. We located a Laundromat but it was full of people doing their wash and we had not the time to sit around. We bought groceries and without being unfaithful to my Stradivari I tried a Czechoslovakian violin in a music store. It was an abomination, which was not surprising since it sold for about fifteen dollars. We had a desperate need for music aboard the *Lady Catherine*, having no radio, so I bought a tin whistle—which, rather than the harp, is certainly the national musical instrument of Ireland. The Irish name is feadóg stáin, meaning "little whistle of tin," and the Irish have a virtuoso technique on this simple instrument. Some years ago I attended a three-day musical festival at Lisdoonvarna in County Clare, and I was vastly impressed by the skill of the performers on the tin whistle. The tunes played were all jigs and reels, but they called for fingering and breath control of the highest quality. But there wasn't a harpist to be seen the day of my visit and that was sad, for when Giraldus Cambrensis visited Ireland in the thirteenth century, he said many spiteful things about the Irish but was able to admit that they excelled everyone in playing the harp.

Actually the harp is not a folk instrument. It is an instrument of the court—of kings then who employed harpists to play before them, as Saul did in Israel and Brian Boru in Ireland. When kings go, harps go also and are replaced by tin whistles and mouth organs, which are instruments country folk can buy and master. The idea that we are to play harps in Heaven stems, I suggest, from the memories of pastoral Israelites who, accustomed to wind instruments made from the horns of sheep and cattle, were delighted during their captivity in Babylon and in Egypt by the tinkling of the harp, and the lavish riches which surrounded the harp player at the Pharaoh's court. Heaven, then, was the court of the Pharaoh, and the harp the instrument we will play when we get there.

Well, with the shopping done, and Tom back with us, with several of his mother's loaves of bread, we started up the river again, and after a little journey found it opening before us into the lovely island-studded expanse of Lough Ree, which may mean the Grey Lake and not the King's Lake as is often held. This translation was given me many years ago by a newspaperman in Athenry who had the best filing system I have ever seen. It consisted of a series of those expansive but shallow drawers in which draftsmen store their vast sheets of paper and the flatened tools of their profession.

In such drawers my newspaper friend had the whole of the newspaper file—clippings about every kind of thing in the world, together with announcements of notable dinner engagements of a hundred years ago, and some coming up next Saturday. In half an hour's thoughtful and educational rummaging he could produce anything you wanted. What I wanted at that time was direction to the La Tène stone, a remarkable carved pillar quite short and, I believe, plainly phallic, which lies nearby.

In searching for a map which would guide me, my friend produced an invitation to a dance in Dublin to celebrate the prowess of the Enniskillen dragoons on the field of Waterloo, the details of an auction of mixed farm stock to be held in July, 1846, a recipe for baking potato cakes, and a letter from a newspaper correspondent in America attesting that several tribes of western Indians were found to speak a language not far removed from Aramaic, pointing to the possibility that they were members of the lost tribes of Israel. (I think that particular letter was a favorite of country newspaper editors in the 1840s and was probably written by one of their staff as a "filler"—to take up four or five inches of space which would otherwise be blank.)

Anyway my Athenry newspaper friend, in half an hour's delightful rummaging through the social events of a century and a half, finally produced a map which guided me to the La Tène stone and with it produced the information that Lough Ree is not Lough Nari (Lake of the Kings), but Lough Airgead, meaning Silver Lake and, by extension, Grey Lake. I would hasten to add he is the only man I know who has ever advanced this derivation, and I am nowhere near sufficiently versed in Gaelic to argue on one side or the other.

"You'll see that the water has a grayish tinge," he said, and that was true enough.

The waters of Lough Ree *have* a gray tinge, which may have something to do with the strata over which the river flows into the lake, but I do not know the geology of the place. It is, however, one of the most delightful of Irish lakes. It has a gentler appearance than Lough Derg and its tiny islands, each with its own ruins, are little verdant gems, where ferns and blackberries and sedges grow so thick that it is almost impossible to get through them. Indeed, on some of the tiny islands, walkways must be cut through this almost tropical growth leading to the local ruins of a little oratory or chapel or monk's cell.

On Hare Island, at the southern entrance of the lake, are the ruins of a tiny church founded, it is said, by St. Kieran even before Clonmacnoise, and at Inchcleraun on the northern side of the lake is what remains of a monastery founded by St. Dairmait in 540 A.D. with the relics of the usual cluster of churches, six in all. The name means Clothra's Island, and Clothra was the sister of Queen Maeve, whose mountain fort provides the name for the Knockmealdown mountains. The queen is said to have been killed on the island by a stone thrown by an enemy while she was bathing.

There was about Lough Ree, on the day that we sailed into it, an almost mystical mood—a stillness of air and of water as if a spell had been put upon the whole place in anticipation of a miracle. The water was so quiet that the bow wave of the *Lady Catherine* could be seen as a tiny dark thread on the silver surface of the lake far, far away. Two or three fat, gleaming fish leaped in mid lake, making a lazy plop in the silence. The sun shone from a sky of the greatest innocence—blue with mountains of cumulus soaring upward in fat and fascinating mounds.

Apart from the engine noise, which the mind could screen out, there was to be heard only the playing of the water as it slipped past the hull and the musical plop of fish lazily taking a fly on the utterly still surface. Each island in the lake looked upon its own reflection in these enchanted waters, and then the miracle occurred for which all this hushed loveliness was the preparation—for a few seconds there was a change of the light and the whole sky was duplicated in the lake, every snow-white convolution of the clouds, every detail of the blue seas and bays between them; all above found its second self in the quiet water below.

The enchantment lasted for only seconds, and then one tiny puff of warm air riffled the surface of the lake and erased this marvelous duplication of the world.

I gave the wheel to Kevin and went forward to the bow, expecting perhaps to see some magical islet appear out of the enchanted water. And a little later an island did indeed rise out of the depths of the lake.

And we went aground on it.

Chapter 14

The island on which we struck did not rise in trembling grace from the depths of Lough Ree. It lay in plain sight a point and a half off the starboard bow with a tatter of a church visible in the depths of a copse of hazelnut and beech. We were steering a course to pass it a hundred yards off and I, on the bow, was peering into the water, which was a pacifying experience but useless for navigational purposes. All that was to be seen in the water was the reflection of that summering sky overhead. And then, in this reflection, there gently appeared brown and bulbous shapes which I thought to be Caliban-like monsters rising out of the lake. Too late I recognized them as limestone boulders and shouted to Kevin to back off. The *Lady Catherine* crunched gently up on them and with a sort of sigh lapsed into a contented silence.

Dear God, I thought, am I, who have sailed some twenty thousand miles of ocean, many times reefed down to a rag and a bare pole, with spray coming aboard out of the pit of night like iron chains—am I, the survivor of such ventures, doomed to run ashore every hour on the hour on the gentlest sheet of water to be found in the whole of Ireland?

My sons Kevin and Christopher saved their lives by saying not a word, for the fault was entirely mine, and I indulged in that profanity which God permits seamen in moments of stress, for if you think Peter got his nets aboard without its aid, you know neither fishermen nor saints.

My mind relieved and my spirit soothed by this exercise, I went aft. Kevin had prudently put the gearshift in neutral and the engine was doing no more than ticking over. "How much water off the stern?" I asked, and Christopher, taking one of the oars for a leadline, reported four feet. There was then no danger of the prop fouling on a rock, so I got all hands aft, standing on the transom, and put the *Lady Catherine* in reverse. She made a gallant attempt at sucking up all the water that was north of her and pushing it south of her. But her bow did not budge off the boulder on which it was resting. I tried a few more surges in reverse but without effect and then sent Rory and Coco forward (they being lightest) to try to heave off with the oars. No luck. Kevin and Chris and Tom took over but without effect. There was no cure for it. We had to go over the side and heave her off, and I was about to say a prayer that the tide was not falling when I recollected that this was a lake and there was no tide.

Chris and Kevin went over the side first to heave her off, but though they heaved and grunted and did a lot of laughing (they thought the whole thing prodigiously funny), they could not budge her. Tom offered to go but between Tom and large bodies of water the Lord has set a perversity. I am sure that Tom, Kevin and Christopher could have heaved her off, but I was not sure that I could get Tom back on board again. So I went overboard myself, not without some reservations since my strep throat was not entirely gone.

The cool waters of Lough Ree, however, cured it. They also cured Kevin's cold which he had brought, as I am sure you are tired of hearing, from Amsterdam. This is not to be marveled at, for the curative powers of the lakes of Ireland, the greater number of which have been blessed by one saint or another, have been known to the people for hundreds of years.

There is one rather obvious thing which you must do in refloating a boat which has gone aground and that is walk carefully around her and find out where the deep water is. It isn't necessarily dead astern, for boats aground have a tendency to slew around. In our case, the deep water was off the port quarter. Once this was ascertained, it was not much trouble to take the *Lady Catherine* by her chine strake or its Fiberglas equivalent and, lifting and heaving, move her inch by inch into the depths. She was floating in a few moments, confirming my dark suspicion that Kevin and Christopher were determined that if they had to go overboard, they would so arrange matters that I would have to go overboard too.

We climbed back on board, restarted the engine, and backed her off. A moment for a word of caution here if you should find yourself in similar straits. If you must go overboard to heave yourself off, cut your engine. It is appallingly easy to get a foot or a hand in a whirling propeller. Sometimes you can pole off, and sometimes you can just take an anchor off to deep water, set it and then, heaving on the anchor line, refloat your boat.

We had gone aground in trying to pass between the tiny island and the western shore of the lake and had been going up the middle of that passage, which seemed the wise thing to do. It was plain that if there was a passage at all, it was over to the west. So with the *Lady Catherine* just making headway, we set out again toward the Connaught shore. The Shell Guide showed only a few roughly drawn contours of the bottom, but trusting to these, the compass and the benevolence of the water blessed by so many saints, we crawled along and after many moments of tension managed to get to the north end of the lake, to where a landscape of sedges stretched all about to a horizon of low-lying fields beyond. We set the anchor on a gravel bottom in six feet of water, with, lying ahead, a lovely little bay bordered by a field, and to the right an arm of the lake, scarcely two hundred feet in extent, with what looked like the remnants of a cement jetty running down to it.

Then we climbed into the dinghy and sounded the water ahead, watched all the time by a mystified cowherd standing by the water's edge. It seemed to him, no doubt, nonsense that two men in a tiny boat should come into a bay, not rowing but pushing the oars on either side down to the bottom. The dinghy went aground several feet from the shore, and then the cowherd said that the landing place lay up the little arm of water to our right. I went in there. The water was so clear that in places one got the impression that the boat was floating on air. There was enough water for the dinghy all the way to the bit of concrete jetty, so it was possible to step ashore without getting our feet wet.

Tom now announced something of which I was entirely ignorant, for though I buy guides of all kinds when traveling, I rarely consult them. "This is the Goldsmith country," he said. "We could get the bikes ashore and visit the Deserted Village."

"The Deserted Village," I said. "Isn't that in England?"

"It's a real village in Ireland," said Tom. "And not four or five miles from here." Those who teach literature to English schoolboys insist that Goldsmith was an Englishman and the Deserted Village a fanciful place which Goldsmith summoned up to illustrate the effect of the Enclosure Act, which deprived English villagers of their grazing rights and living. Indeed, the Britannica to this day unblushingly proclaims Goldsmith an "English poet playwright novelist and man of letters," as it proclaims the statesman Burke an Englishman, though right below that listing there is another Burke who was a notorious criminal and is admitted to have been Irish.

Well, we are used to this curious scholarship in Ireland, so I was delighted to hear, helping to balance the score, that England's Sweet Auburn is an Irish village by the name of Ballymahon.

Off we went, having first got the bikes ashore in one of the more audacious feats of small-boat navigation since Bligh's voyage. They were all piled in the middle of the five-foot dinghy, with Kevin at the bow and Christopher at the stern. With three centimeters of freeboard and not a hair more, they were brought ashore. The cowherd liked the bikes. He liked them so much, for as I have told you they were of gold and of red, that though his cows were bawling to have their udders relieved, and although they crowded at the end of the field and wailed like banshees at the gate to be let out into the milking sheds, he stood and examined the bikes and asked what they would cost if a man should take it into his head to buy one of them new. I believe that, having missed my castle, I could have swapped a bike for a Jersey (full of milk), but I passed up this opportunity. Tom told him how much the bikes retailed for, and the cowherd told us how to get to Goldsmith's Deserted Village along a cow track that met up with the road a quarter of a mile away.

We had a lovely bike ride. During my boyhood I lived for a while in Hampshire, England, and in that part of Hampshire which is close to Winchester. This countryside here was quite as soft and rural as that—it was in fact the most English kind of countryside I have come across in Ireland. The hedges were of hawthorn and the trees about, beeches, oaks and elm. Wild carrot (Queen Anne's lace), harebells and vetches with their purple flowers grew along the footing of the hedge, and above the sunny slope of a hill I heard a skylark, strident and melodious, in the blue sky.

There were little hills and small streams tinkling in the grass and little bridges, and blackberry brambles and here and there deeps of fern and of rush and iris. A chaffinch flew along the hawthorn hedge for a while beside me, and a young thrush with enormous endeavor managed to flutter over a bush at the approach of my bike. It wasn't hard to believe at all that I was approaching Auburn, for this was the countryside that Goldsmith, for all his travels, loved above all other places. There is a reason why this country-side is so English too, for it was the land of the Englishry; the grass-rich, lush central plain of Ireland from which the Celts were driven and the land handed over to their conquerors.

These, like all invaders, brought with them the style and plants of home, and made in this fertile part of Ireland as much of England as they might. To that extent Sweet Auburn is English. It is here that inns have names in the English fashion, and the inn of Auburn, which, as I have said, is really Ballymahon, was the Three Jolly Pigeons (remember *She Stoops to Conquer*?). It is as English an inn as can be conjured, to be ranked with The Bear and Ragged Staff (the badge (not coat) of both Warwick and Northumberland) and The Swan with Two Necks. (The latter should be really the Swan with Two Nicks. Swans were kings' birds, but a swan with two nicks in its bill belonged to some privileged person other than the king.)

So it was through England-in-Ireland that we traveled on winding country lanes, tarred now, and stopped at a little inn to inquire our way. There were three in the bar, a lady and two men, and they emerged into the warm sunlight, great glasses of Guinness in their hands, to examine us and our magic bicycles in the easy way of the Irish and to wonder that a man of my years, bearded and with a bit of a paunch, should be riding a bicycle around the lanes of Ireland. We were headed for Pallas, the reputed birthplace of Goldsmith when his father was vicar (Church of England) hereabouts. We came to it at last through a

gate and along a straight avenue of trees so typical of
eighteenth-century landscaping.

There was only a ruined wall covered with ivy, and
long grass growing thick about it. On the wall was a
plaque proclaiming that here was born Oliver Goldsmith;
childlike, ugly, vain, generous, innocent, wise Oliver Goldsmith. It is surprising all the adjectives which can be applied to him. Not one of them encompasses him, but all
belong to his nature, which was as changing as his native
weather. His genius was that of openness and it is this
which made him the most human of literary figures. All
his contemporaries loved him, for his pretenses were those
of a child playing dress-up, and he could not really be
anything but innocent.

"Is your mind easy?" a friend asked him as he lay
dying.

"It is not," said Goldsmith, and those were his last
words.

On the day that he died, Sir Joshua Reynolds flung
away his pallette for he could paint no more for a while,
and Edmund Burke burst into tears. Here we were then,
in the long summer evening of Ireland to which Goldsmith
had so often wished to return, at the place of his birth;
and while we looked at the ruins in their coat of ivy Mr.
Patrick Maleady came from his house to tell us more about
the great man.

Mr. Maleady is the Boswell of Goldsmith. He is such
an authority on the poet that he has friends and corre-
spondents in every part of the world all interested in
Goldsmith. He can recite *The Deserted Village* from start
to finish, taking it up anywhere as the fancy strikes, and
he gives to each verse exactly the same cadence so that
it becomes a kind of a chant. I thought to match verses
with him, for *The Deserted Village* was one of the loves
of my schooldays, but I was no match for Mr. Maleady

and in any case I kept getting entangled in Gray's "Elegy in a Country Churchyard."

We chatted a good hour with Mr. Maleady, who showed us his stupendous collection of postcards from, I believe, every country on earth (itself a testament to the universal popularity of the poet) and then produced an edition of, I think, 1824 of *The Deserted Village* and another of Goldsmith's *History of the Earth*, written in the days when the poet was a bookseller's hack. Even Goldsmith's hack work has a tender charm, and if you feel I linger too long with the man, it is because I love him.

I wish his mind had been easy when he died.

Chapter 15

It took the most careful navigation the following morning to nurse the *Lady Catherine* back into the main channel of Lough Ree. The channel lay scarcely a mile from the place we had anchored, but with all the twisting and winding we had to do to avoid suspicious water, we were a full hour reaching it, on a splendid day of glorious sunlight.

Once in the channel we ran almost immediately into a rescue operation. There was an island on the western shore of the lake thrusting out toward the channel, and a small power cruiser had gone ashore there. Three other boats were circling around. The law of the sea and of all waters is that you must stop to help any craft you see in trouble. It is an old law going back to the days of Charlemagne, and it is observed by all but churls. Although there were plenty of rescuers available we stopped to inquire whether we could be of aid. We had no sooner done so than the other boats took off, leaving the stricken boat to us alone. You are aware if you have reached this far in this book that I am an expert in going aground. I had already gone aground bow-first, stern-first and by the waist, and I wasn't going to take the *Lady Catherine* in and risk going aground again.

"Chris and I will go with the dinghy, Dad," said Kevin. "You keep in deep water." So I jilled about outside the buoys while the boys rowed over to see what could be done. The cruiser had seemingly gone aground at speed for she was in something like a foot of water. The skipper and his wife, a young Swiss couple, were aboard; and, with Christopher in the water on one side and Kevin on the other, he horrified me by starting his engine and putting it in gear. Kevin said something firmly and the engine died immediately.

It was but fifteen minutes' work for the two boys to get the cruiser afloat. They pushed it into deep water, headed it in the right direction, and got clear of it before the skipper opened up his engine and took off, towing his dinghy by the side. Then Kevin rowed back to me while we watched her.

The cruiser made a wide circle at high speed, and the dinghy over the side promptly swamped. The skipper stopped the engine and attempted to pull the dinghy, with about a ton and a half of water in it, on board. Kevin, who is a mild and generous young man, said we should help them once more, so I put the *Lady Catherine* alongside, Kevin stepped onto the cruiser and, having emptied the dinghy, got it aboard. Then he came back to the *Lady Catherine* and we set off up the lake again. The next shipwreck for that skipper, I am sure, was only a few hours off. But lest I seem condescending, I realized that on my past performances, the same might be true of me.

We left Lough Ree at Lanesborough, a town whose name testifies to the Englishness of the countryside. Its Gaelic name is Beal Atha Liag (the Ford Mouth of the Pillar Stone), which suggests that there was a crossing here, from the earliest time, over the river which divides Ireland east and west. There is a bridge of nine arches across the river here. It is built of the universal limestone and pleasant to see in the sunlight with the swifts skimming over the river for flies and the trout hunting the same flies in little leaps and swirls from the waters below. Beyond Lanesborough at Teamonberry we came to a large lock and, having passed through this, we tied up to a small quay by the side of the river, being but five miles from Longford, where we could reprovision the boat and do some exploring.

Longford is another very English name, but in this it is deceptive. "Long" is Gaelic for ship, and Longford means "Port of the Ships," for it was here that the Vikings established a stronghold from which to raid the country around, access for their ships being obtained up the Camlin river, now but a tiny stream. There is a puzzle in how the Vikings got their ships so far up the Shannon into the very heart of the land. Close to the mouth of the river at Limerick, there is a big drop over rapids. Just below Clonmacnoise there is another piece of very bad water with rapids and limestone boulders. How did they get their huge vessels past these two areas of bad water? Possibly by felling trees and using the trunks as rollers to haul their ships over the rapids. Hundreds of slaves would be required for this work. Perhaps they could pass up and down the areas only in the winter months, when the Shannon was swollen with rain. The wet grass of Ireland might provide a third explanation. It was without a doubt as wet and as lush then as it is now, and given enough man- or ox-power, it would not be too difficult to haul a longship overland past the bad stretches.

We put the bicycles ashore at Teamonberry and we set out in good spirits for Longford, five miles off, forgetting that Irish miles are longer than English miles as are all measures of land in Ireland, a device of great benefit to alien landlords granted land. Longford lay closer to six miles from Teamonberry than five, and two of those miles were a gentle uphill slope which provided me with rather more exercise than I had looked for. Yet the ride was enormously pleasant and all in all (provision being made for sudden showers of rain) I can think of no holiday more pleasant than a bicycle ride about Ireland.

One of the great joys is the lack of automobile traffic. One is not constantly hugging the side of the road, precariously maintaining balance, while a procession of cars swishes past within inches. The cyclist has the liberty of the roads, which are good. This one was of tar macadam with a patina of cow droppings, spread very thin, for we were still in cattle country. This unusual covering stretched from Teamonberry to Longford, and probably for many miles beyond, and, it being something scarcely ever seen in the United States, where people and cows do not occupy the same worlds, it was of great interest to my sons and me.

I told them what stories I knew of this material and of how the British Army, during the Second World War, had used donkey droppings to utterly disrupt Rommel's communications in North Africa. In case you have not heard it, the story goes as follows:

A land mine was needed for use on roads in North Africa, but since it would be employed by civilian sympathizers of the Allies, it had to be simple and in a form which could be placed in the open and not recognized. Now in North Africa in those days, and perhaps even now, the commonest form of transport was by donkey and the roads of North Africa were then littered with donkey droppings.

Some genius decided that a land mine looking like a donkey dropping would be the ideal weapon of sabotage, and a study of the donkey droppings of North Africa over a distance of fifteen hundred miles was undertaken, samples being sent to London, carefully identified as to locality, so that texture and color (dependent on local diet) could be matched. Small mines sufficient to wreck a truck were then built in the required shapes.

The plan worked to perfection. The use of these mines made every donkey dropping in North Africa over a thousand miles and more suspect, and Rommel's transport was greatly slowed because of the need for inspecting every pile encountered by every vehicle that passed. Indeed the mines themselves, once used, were scarcely needed—the authentic article falling under such heavy suspicion that it could not be passed without being inspected by a mine detector. Thus the patient ass struck a blow in defense of democracy, but you will not find a statue to a donkey anywhere in the world—such is the ingratitude of man.

With tales such as this, and an account of how beneficial cow pads are in treating rheumatism of the feet, and how the replacement of draft horses on farms by machinery led to an increase in the demand for artificial fertilizer, the long haul to Longford went by pleasantly enough.

I must pause a moment to pay tribute to the silence of Irish roads. In the intervals between our talks, so great was the silence, because of the absence of traffic, that we could hear the soft whirring of the spokes of the wheel through the air, the little patter the tires made on the road, the bright notes of blackbirds, startled in the hedge as we swept by. I could hear the creaking of my bicycle chain, which because of exposure to rain needed a drop of oil, and the tiny drumming noise, a pianissimo roar, if the expression is permissible, which the wind made as it went past my ears. I realized with a pang how much I had missed all these sounds and for how long. We live now in a Niagara of sound from traffic; the tiny sounds, each one of them so enjoyable, are obliterated. So if you really want to hear all these little voices again, which gave wonder to your childhood, then go to Ireland and out into the Irish countryside. There you can still hear a leaf move in the wind.

Irish towns have, almost without exception, a stark look when seen from a distance. They have a convict quality, gray, grim, bleak and stricken, and this to some extent is because they have their backs to the approaching traveler, their faces being turned toward the main street, square, or complex which forms their center. Longford is no exception. Approached on the road from Teamonberry, a sawtooth of rocks lines the horizon capping a lovely green slope across a tiny river. They are grim roofs atop grim buildings and the heart sinks thinking of the bleakness of the people who must inhabit such a place, and the misery of their lives.

It is all, of course, a tremendous deception. For once we got into Longford, having first passed the most ragged beggar I have seen in all my days, the town proved hospitable, comfortable and at ease with the world. The main street we found clean and wide and alive with little shops and pleasant houses. It is only the back of Longford which is so repelling. If I have not mentioned in the past the good nature of Irish automobile drivers, it is certainly time to mention it now. Riding a bicycle one soon discovers that nothing so quickly destroys the finer aspects of the human character as driving a car. The automobile driver looks on everything else on the road as an enemy and cyclists somehow become invisible to him, or, if visible, they form a species which may be killed or maimed with impunity. But not so in Ireland. There the automobile has not yet changed the nature of man for the worse. Black looks, frowns and threatening gestures are unknown, and you may cross a busy road on a bicycle without bringing down on you the wrath of all the motorists in view.

The tolerance of automobile drivers in Ireland for each other is equally remarkable. Clothed in good humor and ease, they are able to get about their little towns with no police or traffic lights directing them. It is a pleasure, I assure you, to drive a car, stopping out of consideration for your fellowmen and not because you are ordered to do so by a red light. It is a delight, a restoration to real living, to know that you can double-park for the few minutes it takes your wife to go into the grocery store, say hello to the saleswoman, get a paper and a bottle of

milk and come out again, without having a dozen drivers
behind you honking their horns and vehemently desiring
the destruction of you and your whole family.

Tolerance. That word sums up the art of civilization,
and you will find it in quantity on the roads of Ireland,
where you can park on any side of the street, facing in any
direction you wish, without fear of fine or frown.

We bought some excellent lamb chops at Longford as
well as bread and milk and walked about the town, leaving
our purchases with our bicycles without the slightest fear.
There is a refreshment in just strolling around a town
and having nothing to do but window-shop. Longford is
a non-tourist town, though it is a fishing center. What was
offered for sale in the shops was then, not of the souvenir
type, but workaday things like coats and boots and
shovels and rakes and teakettles and so on. There were
farmers wearing leather gaiters and cloth caps in the
streets, and sidewalks were for conversation as much as for
walking. Neighbors and friends stood about in little groups
chatting with each other in the lovely sun. Here a patient
motorist waited for another to finish a conversation with
a man on the sidewalk to get a parking place. There a
woman with a pram and two or three children stopped in
the middle of the street to talk to another, and the auto-
mobiles slowed and circled around without a horn being
blown or a window lowered to hurl an insult.

What a nice town Longford is with its cozy hotels fitted
for farmers, and its wide street fitted for driving cattle
to market and its good sidewalks fitted for passing the
time of day with friends. It is an example to the world,
and the cattle are as good-natured as the people, for returning to the boat, we passed through two herds of
them and, though they lowed a little and lowered their
heads, they politely moved aside and let us through.

And so back to the *Lady Catherine* with two glorious
miles of downhill riding in the soft air and then an excel-

lent dinner of lamb chops and potatoes and gravy and good bread and not a single vegetable, thanks be to God. In the evening I walked along the banks of the Shannon and marveled how, in the twilight, the flowers glowed as if they had stored up the light of the sun and were giving it back now. Daisies and white clover glimmered in the dying day and overhead the sky was mild blue and saffron. Moths, themselves possessed of a touch of luminescence, fluttered from bloom to bloom and the river made a restful whisper sliding past the hull of the boat. Then the earth slipped into darkness and only the heavens shone, and I went to my bunk wondering whether in all those planets above there was a single river as lovely as the Shannon.

Chapter 16

We were now getting to the upper reaches of the river and on the following morning passed through three tiny lakes, Lough Forbes, Lough Bofin and Lough Boderg. I will guess the two latter mean the "Lake of the Fair Cow" and the "Lake of the Red Cow." There were red cows in the lough, standing in the shallow water at the edge, chewing their cud and eyeing us with but the ghost of interest. "Lazy cows," Coco had called them and come to the unalterable conclusion that all cows are torpid and move in slow motion. He was mightily surprised here a little later to see a young heifer take off across a field, tail in the air, and clods of dirt flying from her hooves. She had, I think, been bitten by a cleg, or horsefly, though I remember in my childhood being told that when a horse shied or a cow suddenly started galloping, she had seen some evil thing hiding in a rock or bush. The world in those days had many such creatures lurking about, nor are they all gone, for once, sending Coco out for firewood on a dark night, I found him hesitating at the door.

"What's the matter?" I asked.

"There's things out there," he said. So I went with him, and to tell you the truth, we were both nervous.

By Jamestown we had to pass through another lock, which was in charge of a boy of about ten whose name was Bourke. The Bourkes are a great family hereabouts, and the lock at Teamonberry had been also in charge of a

Bourke. For many years the Bourkes have attended these particular locks but our young lockkeeper that morning had his sights on a great venture. We had by now developed a routine for passing through locks. Kevin, Chris and Tom went ashore to handle the boat's lines and help to open the lock gates. Rory, Coco and I stayed aboard to fend the *Lady Catherine* off the lock wall, which also gave me an opportunity of examining the many plants which grow in the stones of the walls.

It was raining a little as we went through this lock and young Bourke, instead of hurrying back to his house, was anxious for information. He had discovered, working with Kevin and Chris, that we were from America, and that name still has a glory and a magic in Ireland, particularly among the young, that should make every American proud. Well, said young Bourke, there was a man from nearby by the name of Boland who had gone to Chicago only a few months ago. Did I know him? I said no, we hadn't met, but America was a very big place. He didn't seem to quite believe that. Ireland is a big place too, when you're ten, and yet it is known that there's many a man in Galway has run into a friend in far away Dublin. America, I explained carefully, was very much bigger than Ireland, and Los Angeles, where we came from, was, for instance, about two thousand miles from Chicago.

Young Bourke considered this for a while. "Well, is it a *good* place?" he asked, and I knew from the emphasis he put on the word *good* exactly what he meant. He meant, was it a place that a man had a reasonable chance of earning his living? I assured him that it was. It was easy to earn a good living in America, the pay was good, and the people were friendly.

"Are you glad you went there yourself?" he asked, for he knew I was born in Ireland.

"I am," I replied seriously, and pointed out that I had been able to raise my family of six children in America, that I had a nice house and we were all doing well and I had arrived in the country hardly knowing a soul. He said no more than that, having now some deep thinking to do. In ten years' time perhaps there will arrive in New York or Philadelphia or Chicago a young man called Bourke from the banks of the Shannon who has decided that opening and shutting lock gates on the river isn't enough of a life for him. The way he worked so seriously in the rain, I think he will be an asset to the country.

We were approaching Carrick-on-Shannon now, which is in the headwaters of the river and, as Tom pointed out, not too far from Sligo. This remark conveyed no particular significance to me until Tom mentioned that there were races at Sligo, when suddenly Kevin and Christopher became mightily interested. We docked at a new marina on the east bank of the river and got the bicycles overboard to explore the town and find out about Sligo and the races.

Near to Carrick-on-Shannon lies Carrowkeel, which is not a town but a hill. There, sixty years ago, Professor R. A. MacAlister, E. C. Armstrong and H. Lloyd Praeger, struck by the strange shape of the hilltop, undertook some digging. They found fourteen burial cairns, two ruined dolmens and a group of fifty circular stone foundations which proved to be the remains of a prehistoric village. They entered some of the burial cairns and found not just square burial chambers but elaborate cruciform rooms, ten feet high in places, lined with stones and twenty feet long on the longest axis. These were Bronze Age burials, three to four thousand years old, and Praeger, crawling in with a lighted candle, found everything just as it had been when these ancient Celts left the last of their dead in the vault.

The central chamber, where the arms of the cross-shape met, was empty, but in the three chambers giving off from it were burned bones lying on flat stones. There were beads of stone, bone implements made from the antlers of

the red deer, and on a shelf the calcined bones of young
children—perhaps the family of the dead man, slaughtered
to keep him company. The men had been of short stature—
about five foot five inches tall.

I wanted to get to Carrowkeel and went immediately to
the Bórd Failte office to inquire about transportation. It
evolved, however, that Carrowkeel was too far to reach by
bicycle and there was no regular transportation to the
place. The Sligo races proved equally disappointing. There
was a bus to Sligo which we could catch without trouble.
But there were no races. And it was while we were debating these setbacks and wondering whether we could not
make a day of it on the morrow and cycle to Carrowkeel
to visit the graves that time caught up with us.

You will recall that for the Irish, living in eternity, time
has no significance. It had come to have no significance
for us either. I didn't know what day it was or how many
days we had spent so far traveling up the Shannon. Fur-
thermore I didn't particularly care. But time, that imposter,
now thrust his presence brusquely before me. I had to get
the *Lady Catherine* back to Garrykennedy by August
fourteenth and by inquiring at the Bord Failte office we
found that it was now August sixth. Eight days remained
of our water holiday, but I wanted to take the Grand
Canal to Dublin and, if I was going to do that, I couldn't
spend a day bicycling to the Bronze Age graves at
Carrowkeel.

This intrusion of time was a most horrible shock. We
had been mooning lazily about without a schedule and
without a care and now we had to make a plan and start
hurrying. We couldn't afford to go any farther up the
Shannon. That was plain. We were close to the headwaters
but now had to turn back immediately—that very day, in
fact. But first we set out to explore Carrick-on-Shannon,
leaving those handsome bicycles by a railing at the en-

trance to the town, certain that there are no bicycle thieves in Ireland.

The town we found to be truly a delight. It was clean and gay and sprightly, decked with flowers and new paint, and entirely enchanting. Hotels and shops are painted in pastel colors and the windows clean and glittering and the doors newly painted with shiny brass knockers and handles. There were shops with fronts of primrose yellow next to shops with fronts of sky blue or pink or snow white. No official group, I am sure, selected those lovely colors to paint the shops and hotel fronts. Individual pride and not local ordinance painted the doors and polished the knockers. It is a very good feeling to be in a town where the people are proud of the place they live in, and how dreadful are those towns where that kind of pride has gone, and drab streets and dowdy shopfronts are left to be groomed by the public service.

Rory and Cormac were still intent upon fishing and we went off to find fishing tackle for them, for they had lost their previous supply. I thought of a rod and line and spoon or spinning bait since we were constantly underway, but although these could be hired, the price of hire seemed to me huge and we settled for tackle minus the rod and reel. I.had serious doubts as to whether it would be possible to troll on the Grand Canal to Dublin, in any case, for Mr. Ryan at Garrykennedy had said that the canal was not much traveled these days and was full of weeds.

We spent only an hour in pleasant Carrick-on-Shannon and then, returning to the boat, headed downstream for we had the long haul to Dublin through many locks. We had to hurry. The junction of the Grand Canal with the Shannon lay many miles downstream at Shannon Harbor, below Clonmacnoise.

Chapter 17

There were at one time two canals linking the Shannon with Dublin, or more accurately, with the River Liffey in the heart of that city. The first of these was the Grand Canal, which took a slightly southerly route, entering the Shannon about midway between Lough Ree and Lough Derg. It was built toward the end of the eighteenth century, which century was the era of canal building all about the western world. Canals were, of course, ousted by railroads, which came along a little later, as railroads are now being ousted by superhighways and skyways.

In the days of the canals roads were so bad in many parts of the civilized world that horses were drowned in morasses which lay across them.

The second of the canals linking the Shannon with the Liffey and Dublin was built to spite the first. On the board of the first canal, the Grand Canal, were many men of wealth and blood, but among them was a humble and retired cobbler, who had invested heavily in the canal; invested so greatly, in fact, that he was elected to the company of governors. The others on the board, however, treated him miserably, thwarting all his suggestions, snubbing him, and neglecting to inform him of meetings.

After some years of this treatment, the cobbler lost his temper and planned his revenge. He sold out his shares and in very short order organized a company to build a rival canal, to the north, to be called the Royal Canal. The canal was built (though at enormous costs) and opened with great ceremony. It certainly took away a great deal of the trade formerly carried on the Grand Canal. However, it was never as prosperous as the cobbler had hoped, nor did it put his rival company out of business, and he lost his whole fortune on the venture.

The Royal Canal, alas, is no longer in operation. It was still operating in 1949 when L.T.C. Holt wrote his definitive and engaging work, *Green and Silver*, about traveling on Ireland's waterways in a boat. We examined part of the canal at Longford and found it choked with weeds, the locks fallen into decay and one stretch filled in.

We, intent on traveling on the Grand Canal, went south at an unseemly rush, that monster Time having intruded into our paradise, and it is with shame that I record that we stopped only at Athlone to pick up mail. Yet there was one great sight for us in that sweep down the river and the lake—the ruins of Clonmacnoise laid out in the sunlight on their hilly meadow—the two round towers, the tiny churches, the sculptured Great Crosses.

So fast did we go that in one day we had reached Shannon Harbor on the Grand Canal, having negotiated two locks on the canal to get there. The lockkeeper was Mr. James Connally, surely the most obliging man in all the world. Judge of this for yourself. We arrived at the first lock at the entrance to the Grand Canal at half past seven in the evening, and so hardly expected that anybody would be on duty, let alone willing to let us through. But out bustled Mr. Connally in his shirt-sleeves, and with the aid of my sons got the lock gates open and us through. The next lock was a little distance off—half a mile, I think. He got on his bicycle and went up to it and was waiting there for us when we arrived. There was still another lock at Clonony Bridge, a mile away, and Mr. Connally wondered whether it would be convenient for us to wait until the morning to get through that, as it was now beginning to

get dark. He made the suggestion with the greatest courtesy and, had we said we were in a desperate hurry to
get through that third lock, I haven't the slightest doubt
that he would have got on his bicycle again and gone off
to open it for us. But we said that we were delighted to
have been allowed through the locks already opened and
would rest at Shannon Harbor that night.

Between Dublin and Shannon, there are thirty-six locks
in all and a fee for passing through them. The fee was not
much, but Mr. Connally advised skipping the last eight
locks in Dublin itself. Better, he advised, to tie up in the
canal and go into Dublin on our bicycles. We took his
advice and did not pay the fee for the last eight locks
and learned later that the Dublin urchins love to board
boats as they go through the locks, and they also like to
amuse themselves by spitting on the decks of boats as they
pass under bridges. (At fifty-five I call that reprehensible,
but at ten I was pretty good at it myself.)

So through the first two locks of the Grand Canal we
went and tied up to the bank of the canal in Shannon
Harbor, which is a gaunt place, dominated by a ruined
hotel of monstrous size and some lugubrious workshops
and warehouses, whose vast gray walls bear the lichens of
age. The hotel, square and gray as a prison, is not merely
ruined. It is destroyed. Not a window remains in it or a
door or a floor. The roof is all gone. Only the walls stand,
but once it was a fine building in the Georgian style, the
scene of many banquets and dances and of many tears also;
for Shannon Harbor, though in the middle of Ireland, was
one of the great emigration ports of the country. Emigrants to America took the canalboat from Dublin to
Shannon Harbor, and from there were carried by coach
to Galway or perhaps to Sligo or to Limerick. There they
took ship to New York or Philadelphia or Boston, and
some of the sadness of their partings seems to lie over
Shannon Harbor to this day.

The ruined Grand Canal Hotel at Shannon Harbor was deliberately destroyed to avoid payment of taxes. The roof was removed, the floors taken out, the staircase even taken down, and you look through the front door into a vast coffin, appalled that what appears so substantial from outside should be, within, entirely a void.

Ireland is full of ruined buildings, some of historic importance but the greater number of them of little concern. Nobody ever pulls anything down, and abandoned houses and warehouses, barns and cottages are found in every village and along every highway. Abandonment is indeed the Irish method of disposal. I remarked on the abandoned car at the entrance to Portumna, and here in the canal was an abandoned boat, which had sunk by the bank, only the bow breaking the surface. It will be there ten years from now, I am sure, and until it has disintegrated.

We spent the night at Shannon Harbor, in the shadow of that derelict hotel, and early the next morning Mr. Connally was there to open the next lock gate for us and bid us Godspeed.

"If you hurry you can just make it to Dublin and back in time," he said for we had told him of our deadline for returning the boat. But he must have known even as he said this that you cannot hurry by boat in a canal. Three miles an hour is canal speed. It was the speed at which horse-drawn barges were towed along the canal towpaths and even with a self-propelled boat, not much more can be managed. The trouble is the lack of sufficient water, as I explained previously. If I revved the engine up, there was only the slightest increase of speed, but the boat dug a great hollow, as it were, in the water on either side. It produced a prodigious quarter wave which inundated the banks of the canal, threatening heavy damage.

So we went toward Dublin at half-throttle, with the west wind at our backs, and all about a landscape as green as a billiard table. Clear across the center of Ireland we went out of the cattle country and into the bog country. And when we were about in the middle of Ireland, there was not a hill or a mountain range or a tree in sight. The diesel engine drummed, the cows stared, the swans panicked and let us by, and we went from nowhere to nowhere to nowhere in this dreamlike journey, punctuated only by the need to pass through locks or bridges.

Chapter 18

On the first full day of our canal journey, by dint of sheer plugging, we passed through sixteen locks and this gave me ample opportunity for studying the plants which had taken root in the lock walls. These plants are to a degree amphibious, for they spend some time under water—some of them deep under water—while the lock is flooded. Their roots are very deeply set between the stones to prevent their being washed away, for the water entering the lock is turbulent and tended to fling the *Lady Catherine* from side to side. After so many inundations it is surprising that there is still earth in the walls for the roots to feed upon. Yet these plants flourish, and botanists seeking something unusual can on the Grand Canal make the acquaintance of diving dandelions and diving Ranunculus, for such they certainly were.

The dandelions I could only tentatively identify as *Taraxacum paludosum*, which is a variety that flourishes in damp places. Dandelions are curious plants in that they set their seeds without pollination. They are self-fertilizing and so do not interbreed. They are also hard to distinguish one from the other—certainly difficult for botanical amateurs like myself. But the lockkeeper told me that they produce their flowers and their seeds—the famous dandelion clock with which children play blowing games all over Europe and America—without interference from the water. He could not tell me, however, whether the seeds of the diving dandelions are waterborne or whether they break loose only when above the surface and caught by a flurry of wind.

I am not sure how old the Grand Canal is, but I would hazard that many of its locks are well over a century old. It is possible then that the dandelions on the walls have been reseeding themselves for a hundred years. I can visualize an excellent paper on the subject titled, "Dandelions of the Irish Locks—A Study in Vegetable Parthenogenesis." It is possible they differ from lock to lock—maybe even significantly.

Next after the dandelion I found the Ranunculus fairly common. They were all, I think, *Ranunculus aquatilis,* which put out a white flower, though this was not the blooming period. I could reckon on finding one or two specimens in each lock close to the lock gates. Here and there, though not in every lock, were small bushes which looked like beech, but my botany is not good enough to make a positive identification.

There was one plant on the locks I could not identify— a grass with fine hairlike blades, several inches in length. That I could not identify it, I hasten to add, was a reflection on my botany and not an indication that the grass was rare, for my meager store of knowledge is picked up pack-rat-like—at random. I could not find this grass, however, in the pastures around, though it may well be there.

To complete this vegetable survey, I examined the enormous wooden levers by which the lock gates are opened and closed and found them to be of greenheart, a South American tropical wood highly resistant to weather and to weathering. It was often used for the pilings of piers and is, I think, heavier than water. Greenheart is great wood for fishing poles and a sort of cousin wood—purpleheart—is, I think, the purnambuco wood out of which the best violin bows are made, though they are fashioned now of Fiberglas also, and I am told that material serves excellently.

On the afternoon of the first day of voyaging up the Grand Canal my sore throat and fever returned. Rory had recovered from his attack but I was not so fortunate and my lungs began to hurt also. I am told that the lungs actually are insensible to pain, but in this I am a medical exception, for mine hurt abominably and made me quite bad tempered, so that I snapped at Kevin and Christopher when, doing their best, they still bumped the side of the boat against the limestone channel under low bridges or snapped at Rory and Coco when they were not quick enough in fending us off in the locks. I am ashamed of this now, but there is no use pretending that my behavior would be any the better in like circumstances in future. Such virtues as I have when healthy disappear when I am sick, and I am left to contemplate the prospect that what I need to attain Heaven is not a priest but a doctor.

When we got to Tullamore I was too miserable to be about and went off to my bunk, handing the boat over to Kevin. We stopped at Tullamore to refuel and to let Tom ashore for he, like the Hobbits' Gandolf, wished to disappear again. Tullamore I did not see. It is notable about the world as the home of a fine whiskey called Tullamore Dew, and the whiskey has endeared itself even to teetotallers like myself for its motto, "Give Every Man His Dew." Not finding a fuel dock handy in the harbor of Tullamore, which is reached through a narrow passage off the canal, Kevin took the boat on up, seeking to put in as many miles on the water-road to Dublin as possible.

"You'll find a place to refuel eight miles up the canal," Kevin was assured at Tullamore, and he believed this. But, alas, the assurances of my countrymen are not always to be relied on, for the Irish tend to believe that the worst never happens. This is remarkable for, in Ireland, the worst is what happens all the time, but the Irish are so used to this I suppose they don't notice. The worst in our case was to run out of diesel fuel halfway to Dublin, so I was anxious to find a source of supply as early as possible. About eight miles up the canal from Tullamore we came to Philipstown, where there was a little landing quay and a bridge across the canal. Two men were standing by a tractor here, and since tractors have to run on fuel, we landed to inquire if there was any diesel available.

It was the quiet of the evening now, the time when all the noises of the day have fallen to a hush and people speak in lowered tones, and from the hedges you get an occasional half-frightened chirp from a bird and then a tense sort of listening. So we approached the two men in this mystical hour with gentleness.

One does not come directly to the point in the country in any case. One talks of things in general and only gradually approaches the crucial topic. So I remarked, throwing a clove hitch around a convenient post, that it was a lovely evening, and one of the men said that it was and that it had been a lovely day all together. Kevin patted the dog—in Ireland in the country there is always a dog about—and I eyed the tractor and remarked that in my day all had been equipped with metal cleats which tore up the road very badly. The older of the two men remembered this condition, and how the cleats used to fill with mud. The rubber tires, he said, were more efficient.

The old tractors ran on kerosene. You started them on petrol and then when the engine was hot you switched to kerosene. I mentioned this to the two men and gathered in return the information that tractors run on diesel fuel now.

This was the time to mention my own need of fuel, but the opening was too obvious, so we went on to talk about fishing in the canal. One of the men showed Rory and

Cormac (who whenever we stopped fell immediately to fishing) how they might take a big pike if they would row slowly down the canal with a hook baited in a certain manner. They tried but without success, though they had glorious moments of pleasure hoping for an enormous fish.

The talk turned to other parts of Ireland. I mentioned having visited Roundstone in Galway (Cnoc na ron—the seals' stone) and meeting the King family there. They are a fishing and farming people who rented us a house. Did I really know little Jackie King then, from Galway? one of the men asked. I said I did.

"He's in Dublin now," he replied. "He's fishing in Dublin and doing well for himself." The last time I met him he was a shy, thin little boy playing football in the street with Kevin. That had been a long time ago. Men had not yet set foot on the moon.

Eventually I mentioned my need for diesel fuel and it was suggested that I might find some at the store in the town. There was only one store and the town was but a meager row of houses.

The store did not stock diesel but there was some available for the farm tractors. It was agreed that I could put "tractor diesel" in the boat. Did I have a container? I did not. Did I have a tundish? A tundish? That word which astonished Joyce's teacher in *A Portrait of the Artist as a Young Man* was produced without the slightest affectation —a fossil of a word dating back to the fourteenth century and still alive here. A tundish is a funnel and I hadn't one but it was thought perhaps we could manage without it.

The man in the store nodded his head and said he would come to the boat with some fuel in a little while. We bought a few groceries—always that good bread—and the fuel turned up twenty minutes later. It wasn't an item stocked for sale at the grocery. We were supplied from the stock of the local farm tractors and we made a tundish out of a newspaper whose headlines suggested that the whole of Ireland would be a bloodbath before the week was out.

No one seemed concerned about this and when the refueling was done, we talked on in the quiet of the evening of the poorness of the potato crop and the ease with which milk may be obtained in the neighborhood. I thought this was the result of the plenitude of cows, but it is the result of the power of fairies.

It seemed that at one time there was a poor widow in the neighborhood on whom the fairies took pity and presented her with a cow. The cow gave an endless supply of milk and the widow was only too glad to give it to anyone who asked for it. But while she was away from her cottage one day, a beggar came along and asked for a little milk and he was refused. Immediately the fairy cow went dry and never produced another drop, though this was by no means the widow's fault. Still, fairies don't reason like human beings and have a quixotic sense of justice. But to this day you can get milk from any farmhouse around Philipstown and not a penny will be asked in payment or accepted.

We paid for the diesel fuel, however, though I had difficulty in getting payment accepted.

Chapter 19

We tied up for the night to the bank of the canal a little past Philipstown, and the following morning, it being Sunday, set out for Mass in the chapel of a school Kevin had located. The whole place was surrounded by a high wall of limestone—enormously high and without handholds or ports through it—and had a grim appearance. We entered a little hesitantly through a gate and found inside a delightful garden with sweet peas and roses and marigolds and Virginia stock in bloom. Beyond the garden was a severe gray building, and we followed others from the village through a door and so came to a chapel scrupulously clean and strangely severe. What kind of school was this?

That part of the congregation which had assembled from the village was in the rear pews, and not knowing who else might be expected, we also took seats in the rear. After a little while there was a subdued and then not-so-subdued shuffling and perhaps thirty boys came into the church and occupied the front pews, leaving a sort of no man's land between the village congregation and the boarders of the school.

The older ones among them wore a uniform of a gold-colored, knitted jersey and corduroy pants. They clattered into their places, hair unruly, their faces pinched and eyes hard. Gradually it dawned on us that this was no ordinary school, nor these ordinary pupils. They were offenders against the law in varying degrees and this was a school for juvenile delinquents. I learned later they could be sentenced to the school for periods of up to two years for offenses varying from stealing motorbikes and cars to robbing houses.

They seemed unruly rather than devout during the Mass, with one touching exception. When the priest said the prayers for the dead, the jostling, the grimacing and the whispering ceased and every cropped head was lowered. There were a lot of dead to be remembered among them, I suppose. After the Mass I spoke to a young priest about the boys. He said they came almost without exception from permissive homes or broken homes—homes where the normal disciplines between parents and children are lacking. They were allowed, with good behavior, to go to their homes for the holidays. Some were drug users. There was a lack of staff and a lack of money. The boys got psychiatric help but more would be useful if funds allowed. The younger ones tended to pick up the vices of the older. There was no helping that. One little fellow, his face all innocence, particularly appealed to me and I asked about him.

"He's only twelve years of age, but he stabbed three of the boys with a dagger made from a spoon handle; one of them his own brother," was the reply.

After Mass we breakfasted aboard and then continued along the canal, leaving the cattle country and entering the Bog of Allen. Bog in Ireland, you understand, is not the same thing as bog in England or bog in the United States. An Irish bog is not a place of water lilies, rushes, watercresses, mudbanks, marsh marigolds and ooze. It is a vast acreage of "turf," which the rest of the world knows as peat. The "turf" is black lower down and chocolate brown on the surface, and it is fibrous and burns with a heavenly scent not unlike well-dried hay. Its botany varies, but in Ireland it is composed largely of bog rosemary (*Andromeda polifolia*) and mosses, sedges, rushes and reeds, though in what quantities and varieties I do not know. These, dying, oxidize and decompose, the decomposition aided by those same anaerobic bacteria and molds that produced the world's vast coalfields at the end of the Devonian era.

Peat, then, is coal in the making, and what is going on at the present time in Ireland, Germany, Canada and the United States is precisely the same process that went on in the Carboniferous period millions of years ago.

Russia has the world's largest deposit of peat with an estimated sixty-five-thousand square miles of the stuff, and Great Britain (that is to say England, Scotland, Wales and the Six Counties of Northeast Ireland) has twice as much as the Republic of Ireland. But they do not use it to the same extent.

The Irish use peat of necessity, for they have no other fuel and they produce about six million tons of it a year, the greater part machine-cut but a good portion cut on the bogs with a special spade called a slán (pronounced slawn). It was on the bog, cutting peat, that I met the former New York City bus driver, you will recall. It takes about six weeks for peat to dry sufficiently to be used as fuel and a warm southwest wind is a great help, and a blessing too in making hay. Did I tell you about the fishermen of Roundstone and the peat? I did not. Well, it used to be the custom to haul the peat from Roundstone to Galway by water on a good-sized boat of a type called a hooker. Such a boat had two masts, was ketch rigged, and could carry a big tonnage. One summer, years ago, the peat was a long time drying, and the fishermen who ran the hooker got tired of waiting for it.

"We'd have time to get to America and back before it's dry," said one.

"Let's do it," said another. "I have a brother in Philadelphia I haven't seen in ten years." They had food aboard and water in plenty, and off they went. They went all the way to America and found out where Philadelphia was but the man's brother had gone to Chicago so they missed him. However, they went on up to Atlantic City and had a spell ashore there and then came on back, and when they pulled into Roundstone the peat was piled up on the quay waiting for them, so they did not lose a penny from the journey. I do not know whether this story is true, but I saw the remains of the old hooker lying in the harbor at Roundstone myself. A good stout craft, she was, with ribs of oak. But the year after I saw her, the weather was wet all summer long and the peat would hardly dry at all, so the people of Roundstone cut up the old boat and burned it in their fireplaces to get them through the winter; for that is the way things go very often in Ireland.

The countryside about, in the journey through the Bog of Allen, was all of one color, a sort of brown green, and it was not long before we would have been highly excited to see a tree. The canal, now very little used, was choked with weeds—chickweed, watercresses, rushes, and in places plants that looked by their curly leaves remarkably like Ranunculus and perhaps they were for there are several species, I think, which will grow partially submerged. I wished very much I had a botanist with me, for the variety of the weeds in the canal was enticing.

I don't suppose the canal is now more than five feet deep, so the sunlight could easily strike to the bottom, and in many parts we were floating over a water garden, so thick was the growth below. This same growth, of course, gave me some concern for my propeller, and I would stop every now and then and put it in reverse to clear it of weed. The clutch was slipping more and more and the engine overheating—in fact the engine was giving me precisely the same trouble that a similar engine on board my yawl *Bahia* had given me.

I knew how to cure the trouble, but I had nothing but

a can opener and tableware for tools. I could, of course, have stopped in almost any town with a garage and had a mechanic tighten up the drive bands for me. But I tend to think of machinery as living and to believe that the ills from which it suffers will in time be cured. Sometimes this happens in ways which I cannot explain, and it is always a good idea with electricity to give it a good thump so that it stops daydreaming and gets on with operating the radio or whatever may be its duty. But the clutch didn't get better. It got worse, and I decided that I would have it fixed when I got to Dublin.

Alas for the lovely Grand Canal of Ireland. It is used by every farmer as a dumping ground for garbage and for offal. There are delightful stretches of water gardens, and others quite foul. We passed the bloated carcass of a pig and another of a calf, both bobbing about among the water lilies and cresses. I made a count of cadavers and in an hour (which would be a distance of, say, three miles) passed twelve, of which, I must admit, eight were fish caught, killed and discarded to decay in the canal. The other four were so unsavory I will skip identifying them. The canal, being little used, offers a convenient dumping place, yet if tourism by water is to have a future in Ireland this will have to stop. It is surprising to find that despite this dumping, the fish population of the canal is vigorous. We saw schools of roach and, I think, chub in the clear, sunlit water. But there were places too where a green scum coated rushes and other growths, giving warning of what could happen to the whole canal if controls are not imposed.

A great nuisance in the canal were plastic bags, some partially submerged and scarcely visible. These threatened our propeller and after passing over one—they could not always be seen in time to be avoided—it was necessary to go vigorously into reverse to stop the propeller being fouled.

After some hours of plodding up the canal, we saw at last a staggering sight—mountains "fine on the starboard bow" as they say in the best whaling books. It was actually exciting to see the land rise toward the sky, as if it had come alive at last. The mountains were the Wicklows, of which only one or two peaks top three thousand feet. In that flatland they seemed spectacular. Gradually the boglands receded and we came into very English-looking countryside—English in that there were trees and gardens, and the trees were horse chestnuts and oaks and elms. We were entering the area of the Pale—the oldest of the Anglo-Norman settlements in Ireland—where the English influence was and is the strongest.

In case you are unfamiliar with Irish history, the Pale was actually a ditch surmounted by a massive fence (the word has the same root as the word *paling*), its purpose being to provide a sanctuary for the English (Anglo-Norman) invaders. The Pale ran from Dundalk on the coast inland toward Kells and then roughly southward to the Wicklows. Dublin was its axis, and the remains of this ancient defensive fortification are still to be traced, I am told.

Here the culture of England was encouraged, the language gradually became English and the dress and customs of the people also. Beyond the Pale was wild Gaelic Ireland, as it was thought of. But there were times when the kings of England complained that the English of the Pale were more Irish than the Irish—wilder, more rebellious, and more unpredictable. And having said some hard words about Cromwell and his troops earlier, I must even the score now by saying that it was the descendants of these invaders, settled in Ireland, who provided leadership in the Irish struggle for independence when the Gaelic Irish had, like the American Indian, been ground into apathy.

There was another change as we entered this area of the ancient Pale. The building material of the lock walls had

all been so far of gray limestone. Now we found walls
of granite, having passed out of the limestone area, and
that in itself helps to account for the difference in the
landscape and vegetation, for granite does not soak up and
hold water as limestone does. Granite also, coming from
the bowels of the earth, is the primary building material of
mountains.

How very nice it was to find again the monotony of
the bog replaced by gardens and leafy lanes; to see the
land rise and fall and watch the blue cloud shadows fleet-
ing over the Wicklows. We had passed one of Nature's
doors and entered a new land and a pleasant one. We
journeyed through it for an hour or two, reveling in
places where trees actually grew alongside the canal, and
then pulled into a quay before the twelfth lock, where
there was a hedge of climbing roses and beyond it a little
grocery store. There were mooring cleats here on the quay
and one or two other boats tied up, so we knew we could
stop here.

We reached this point—the end of the canal as far as
we were concerned—too late in the day to go into Dublin;
but we were up and off early on our bicycles the following
morning. The distance was but ten miles or so and the
first half of the ride was as pleasant as could be imagined
—along small roads, well paved, through high hedges of
hawthorn and hazelnut, and with long grass growing on
the sides. The sun shone and the birds sang and I felt remarkably strong and healthy and paid no attention at all
to what my muscles would feel like that evening after a
twenty-mile bicycle ride.

After four miles of this very pleasant sort of riding, our
little road turned into the main Dublin road, and also
immediately into the city's suburbs. It was a good wide
road and although I had never approached Dublin from
the land side, we found our way to the Liffey and then
across a bridge to Phoenix Park and so on down along the

quays to O'Connell Street—lovely, wide O'Connell Street, with the flowers in baskets on the bridge and the statues of all the people in the middle, except Lord Nelson, who was toppled with his column some years back.

I wanted to go to the National Museum, but the museum was shut. I tried the National Library. That too was shut for cleaning, which, I believe, is undertaken extensively each summer. But the Library of Trinity College we found open and off we went then, Kevin, Christopher, Rory, Cormac and I, to that great treasure-house of leather-bound tomes stacked in racks to the ceiling. Here in a case was the diary of Dean Swift, written in his crabbed hand; there, a manuscript of Goldsmith; and beside it the diary of Theobald Wolfe Tone, opened at the page where, contemplating the prospect of being "hanged, drawn [disemboweled] and quartered [cut into four pieces]," he remarked that so long as the hanging came first he did not give a fig for what followed.

There was one book I wanted to see above all others in the Trinity College Library—the Book of Kells. It is an illuminated copy of the Bible, in Latin, and dates from the seven hundreds. It is said to be the oldest illuminated Bible in existence and was compiled with immense care by many monks, the letters exactly drawn in Gothic script with a quill pen dipped in ink made of the juice of holly berries.

You stand, having taken your place in line, in silence before the opened page, thinking of the long dead monks who filled out the vellum leaves. The involuted lines of the illuminated initials, curling and twisting toward an end that will not end, assure you that this is the symbol of life itself. The end is the beginning. The beginning is the end. The colors are so faded they are like the petals of flowers pressed between the years. They are not colors but the ghosts of colors. They were fresh when Charlemagne had scarcely begun his rule; when Rome still flourished in its eastern empire at Constantinople; and when the New World, north or south, was unknown or, if known, was only a mystic land visited by Brendan the Navigator.

So I stood and when I moved aside, so my sons stood, and as I watched them it was revealed to me that I had at last brought them to the very heart of Ireland. For Ireland does not live by or in the usual matters of history—for power, for land, and for money. There have been struggles aplenty, it is true, over all these things. But beyond these, greater than them, enduring through them, never lost sight of as an objective, has always been in Ireland that other dimension which is not confined in time nor in things, but which found its expression in round towers and little chapels, in monasteries and hermitages, in legends and in myths and in dreams, and right here in the Book of Kells.

I had brought my sons then to the Holy Grail of Ireland—my sons, who were named for Kevin of Glendalough, Christopher, the Bearer of Christ, Cormac, of the Chapel of Cashel, and Rory, last high king of Ireland.

The quest was done. I could go back to California. There was nothing more in Ireland or indeed in all the world to show them.